Praise for *Homeschooling: You CAN Do It!*

With more families considering homeschooling than ever before, Kirsten's resource is essential for the homeschooling book market. The information in this book clearly guides one through the maze of the homeschool experience. Every question that will come up is answered in very easy to understand prose. Even if you have already started homeschooling, nobody has all the answers all the time, but Kirsten's book does. I highly recommend the book for all homeschooling families; it will be your one-stop shop for all your homeschooling questions and challenges.

—*J. Michael Smith, Esq.*
President, Home School Legal Defense Association

Do you love the idea of homeschooling but have no idea where to start? Have more questions than answers? Kirsten has done an amazing job of laying out all the fundamentals and then giving you the confidence to go ahead and execute! *Homeschooling: You CAN Do It!* is definitely a must-read for any parents considering homeschooling, and additionally is a great resource for those already muddling their way through it but still find they have tons of questions. I highly recommend this book!

—*Amber Fox, thehomeschoolinghousewife.org*
author, blogger, and homeschooling mama of seven kiddos

Homeschooling is about so much more than book learning. It really is a lifestyle...one that almost any family can live out. Kirsten's book helps paint a clear picture of what that can look like. She also addresses so many of the challenges that parents face and gives practical ideas on how to overcome them. She makes homeschooling do-able and by doing so, helps bring the confidence that every homeschooling parent longs for.

—*Durenda Wilson, durendawilson.com*
author of The Unhurried Homeschooler

HOMESCHOOLING: YOU CAN DO IT!

ELIMINATE SELF-DOUBT AND GET THE CLARITY, CONFIDENCE, AND SKILLS YOU NEED TO SUCCESSFULLY TEACH YOUR CHILDREN FROM HOME

KIRSTEN MCTERNAN

ॐ

SHELBURNE PUBLISHING

Printed in the United States of America

First Printing, 2018

ISBN: 978-1-7324285-1-5 (paperback)
ISBN: 978-1-7324285-0-8 (e-book)
Library of Congress Control Number: 2018907627

Dedication

To my four precious sons:
Liam, Thomas, Julian, and Shane.
You are my heart
and the reason I'm able to write this book.
You inspire me every day to be my best self,
and you are a joy to teach.

I love you!

Table of Contents

Part II: How to Homeschool with Confidence

Part III: Resources: Sample Charts and Online Links

Foreword

I stood under a large maple tree one afternoon patiently staring at the Sun. I was waiting for the first sliver of darkness to begin its encompassing journey across the face of the Sun. A partial solar eclipse was about to occur, and I was extremely excited. This was my 5th grade science class. The teacher was my mom.

She homeschooled me and my two brothers for four years with love and enthusiasm that affected the trajectory of my life. My fascination with the guiding principles of nature and the unfathomable mysteries of God's creation started unequivocally with my mom's science classes. She was not a scientist by trade. Nor was she formally trained as an educator. She did not have mentors, close friends, or relatives who homeschooled, yet she gave me a personalized education that sustained me through high school, graduate school, and to my current position with NASA. My mom's success as a home educator is not defined by what was lacking but by her enthusiasm, dedication, and faith.

Over twenty-five years after that memorable solar eclipse, I found myself, again, patiently staring at the Sun. This time, I was accompanied by my wife and children. We were at Christian Way Farm near Hopkinsville, Kentucky, which was the point of greatest eclipse for the 2017 total solar eclipse. I had just finished my PhD at Penn State and was on my first assignment with NASA. As the bright disk of the Sun began to disappear behind the Moon, and the familiar disk became a strange, bright crescent (a shape normally reserved for the night sky), I brought my family under the shade of a large tree. We were looking for crescent-shaped images on the ground caused by a pinhole-camera effect as the image of the sky was focused onto the ground below. I first observed this effect in my mom's 5th grade science class under the maple tree. I didn't know what a pinhole camera was at the time. I didn't understand optics. It didn't matter. I was ecstatic at the heuristic, visceral insight that, somehow, light was manipulated by the gaps in the tree's leaves. I knew from that moment on that the flitter of shadows and light rays under all trees during the day was a compilation of images of the sky above. Now, in 2017, I laid down on the ground and let the crescent shapes form on my white shirt. We took a picture and texted it to my mom—my science teacher. The crescent shapes became increasingly thin as the Moon continued its path in front of the Sun. Minutes later: totality. Unfamiliar scenes and indescribable emotions overwhelmed us all. It was almost noon, but it seemed like dusk. There was light, but from a glowing black disk. It was as if a miracle had just occurred. It declared "I am."

My education is, in many ways, bookended by solar eclipses. The first eclipse piqued my interest in astronomical events and taught me the joy of discovery. The second marked the end of my formal education and the beginning of a career researching the environment of the upper atmosphere and low-Earth orbit. But, these eclipse stories and this book are not about me. They are about parents who stepped out in faith to educate their children the way they felt was best for the child. I happen to be a beneficiary of such faith, and you, too, can give this gift to your children. I attribute a large part of my academic success to my mom.

Kirsten (the author, my wife) and I have decided to do the same for our children. Like many parents holding this book, Kirsten wanted to homeschool but did not have the confidence or know where to begin. Looking back at her success and her current abilities, it is ironic to think that she doubted herself—that she questioned the outcome. Now, it seems obvious. She became who she wanted to be.

I hope that, after reading this book and the testimonials at the end, you will feel empowered to educate your own children the way you want to. That, instead of seeing barriers, you will see opportunities. Where there might be uncertainty, you will be a leader. And, where you feel weakness, you will see Christ's strength.

Jesse McTernan, PhD

Acknowledgements

First and foremost, I would like to thank my Lord and Savior, Jesus Christ, who created me with a purpose, gives me hope, and enables me each new day. I'm grateful He blessed me with four incredible boys to love and teach. They are my delight. Liam, Thomas, Julian, and Shane: I love you with all my heart.

To my husband, Jesse: I could not have done this without you. You were the behind-the-scenes, hard-working dad who would get home from working for NASA to entertain our kids and take care of the bedtime routines so I could lock myself in the office to put my thoughts in written form. You also enthusiastically cheered me on, like the time you secretly posted a sign by my computer reading, "Book Writing: You CAN Do It!" It made me laugh, and it became a source of encouragement to me each time I sat down to write or edit. Thank you for believing in me, praying for me, and for choosing to spend your time to help me to achieve this goal, AND—I appreciate all the ways you consistently show your support in the effort to homeschool our boys. I love you!

To my parents who, throughout my growing-up years, strove to give me a top-notch education no matter which country we lived in. You were my advocates and always sought to do what was best for me. You gave me incredible adventures, and you limited TV time which allowed my creativity to blossom. I'm incredibly thankful for that! Thank you, Mom and Dad, for your continual love for me, and for giving me the encouragement I needed to try homeschooling in the first place.

To my writing coach, Scott Allan: thank you for taking the time to listen, encourage, and give me sound advice during both the writing stage and launch process. You helped me navigate the steps needed to self-publish, saving me a lot of time trying to figure it out on my own, and I'm so grateful.

To my editor, Jody: I'm so thankful the Lord put us together for this project! It has been an absolute pleasure working with you. You helped polish my words, gave me honest feedback, prayed for me, and showed continuous joy throughout the whole process. At times, I felt you were more excited about my book than I was! (And that's saying something!)

This book took a team effort to get published. It's self-published, and I needed support to have it edited, formatted, designed, and marketed. I reluctantly (and self-consciously!) put out a GoFundMe request and was able to make this book idea a reality! To all the donors: thank you so much for believing in me!

To all my homeschool friends who shared their experiences in this book: thank you for being transparent and opening the door to your own homeschool for my readers. I appreciate you taking the time to share your helpful knowledge and advice.

To my book launch team: you rock! Thank you for spreading the word, proofing my final edit, and giving me the final push and courage I needed before hitting "Publish"!

And to my readers: thank you for allowing me to have the opportunity to speak into your life through my writing. You are special, unique, designed *on* purpose *for* a purpose, and loved intimately by the Almighty God. Never forget that.

Thank you!

Introduction

Are you interested in homeschooling but feel unqualified, doubting your ability to do it well? Do you want to learn what's actually involved before making this important decision? Or maybe you are currently homeschooling, but you're feeling overwhelmed. Friend, I'm glad you picked up this book! I have been in your shoes, and I understand how it feels to be burdened with this hefty decision and feeling less-than-capable for the task of educating your children.

This book was born after speaking with multiple people over the years who admired how I homeschooled, but who doubted they could do it themselves. I received comments like, "You must have a lot of patience!" or, "I could never do that." While they were intending to be complementary, I felt the weight of their personal discouragement. I wanted them to know that I struggled to believe in myself just like them. I started this homeschooling journey with uncertainty, but God stepped in and allowed my heart to change from struggle to enjoyment, and I progressed as I went. As a result of these conversations, I became passionate about sharing my story to encourage others. I didn't want these parents to settle for less than what they dreamed of for their families. I desired to share hope and allow them to experience the benefits and joys of educating their children. Yes, there have been struggles, too—and while I don't shy away from laying them out in this book so you can learn from them, I hope you'll recognize that with challenges also come rewards and great blessing.

In my own search for homeschool how-to resources, I discovered that while there are several books available on how to homeschool, I didn't find many that were written directly to those who doubt they can do it and that go through the questions of whether or not it's a good fit for their family. Not only does this book attempt to guide you through this important thought process, it does so by establishing the many reasons why homeschooling should be considered.

Furthermore, I have not found much that directly addresses the single parent who is considering homeschooling. Single parents are dear to my heart, as I began my own parenting journey as a single mother. I have several single-parent friends who have been called to homeschool; they are doing it successfully and love it! If you are single, it IS possible for you to homeschool. I have written a section just for you, and you'll receive encouragement from others like yourself who have shared their experiences in the Testimonials section.

For those of you who have already begun the homeschooling adventure, I pray this book will enhance your experience. My aim is to help you cast a clear vision for your family as you become more focused, seek out answers to your questions, manage your daily tasks, and gain fresh ideas. May you also be encouraged and reminded of the reason you decided to homeschool in the first place.

To conclude this book, I have put together a section of testimonials. (It's like getting together with a group of my successful homeschooling friends and interviewing them on the subject. There's a wealth of ideas and encouragement here!) You'll hear from some who were homeschooled growing up, some who are currently homeschooling, and others who are veteran homeschoolers. I want to pass on a well-rounded selection of knowledge and expertise to you so you don't have to start from scratch, while keeping this information as concise as possible. As a busy mom, I understand the longing to read but the lack of time to do it.

Our children are our greatest gifts, and they grow quickly! As parents, we are entrusted with the daily responsibility of making decisions for our children that will affect their future. How your child is educated is one of those decisions with lasting consequences. The choices you make today are creating a legacy for your children for years, perhaps even generations to come.

Friend, you can do so much more than you realize. I pray the Lord will clearly lead you and inspire you to do what is best for your family, while giving you an abundance of strength and wisdom. I never dreamed I would homeschool, but I ended up loving it! I'm here to tell you it is possible—you CAN do it!—and I will provide a number of tools to show you how. I want you to finish this book refreshed, ready to go forth in confidence as you develop your own God-given abilities to teach and nurture your child effectively by the power of His Spirit.

Kirsten McTernan

Part I

**You are stronger than you know.
You've got this!**

Chapter 1

My Story: I Didn't Think I Could Homeschool

My heart leaped out of my chest upon receiving a phone call from the principal of my son's middle school. She was calling to tell me my son was pulled from classes for questioning. He had been witness to an incident involving a gun on school property.

Just two months earlier, I had made the decision to send my son back to public school after five years of homeschooling. I felt he was well prepared for the school environment, but I never imagined he would come face-to-face with a gun. In just two months of being back in public school, there were many episodes that caused me to question whether public school was right for him, but this surpassed them all. Still, I wrestled with the decision. I wanted to make sure that if I pulled him out of public school it was because the Lord was calling me to do so—not because I was afraid.

Seven years earlier, I had decided to pull my son out of public school for the first time. Now, here I was at this pivotal decision again, only this time I had three more children to consider.

Questions and doubts were running through my mind: Do I homeschool again? How will I manage to do it? My son is halfway through 8th grade—do I pull him out mid-year? I can't imagine homeschooling through the high school years!

Similar thoughts had flooded my mind seven years earlier.

❧

I'm excited to share with you my story and experiences, but before I do, I want to give you some background that will help paint the picture of the circumstances surrounding this decision. Like hearing a powerful testimony, learning that this process did not begin with the perfect situation may be encouraging to those of you who think you have to have it "all together" to homeschool.

Back when I was in my early twenties, I was single, attending college in New York City, and living life in the fast lane. I had big career goals: to launch my own business, or to get into the music industry. I was a go-getter and took advantage of every opportunity that sounded appealing to me. Besides attending classes, I was a writer for the college newspaper, dancer on the dance club team, DJ on the college radio station, hair model, held an internship, and worked part time as an event marketing manager. In the evenings, I was a night club promoter.

While it was exciting in the moment, it was void of a relationship with God, and this self-gratifying lifestyle left me empty inside. I devoted all my time and efforts to myself rather than thinking about others. I struggled with intense panic attacks that would strike randomly and make me feel like I was suffocating. I jumped from relationship to relationship trying to fulfill a need for love that only Jesus could satisfy.

Well, the rubber hit the road when, in my senior year of college, I found out I was pregnant. The plans I had for myself came to a screeching halt. Days before I found out I was pregnant I had interviewed with the Sony Music record label. Just after receiving the positive pregnancy test result, I listened to a message on my voicemail from Sony, wishing me congratulations—they had hired me. But I couldn't bring myself to call them back. I was young, confused, and scared. How could I be a mom when I could barely take care of myself? I had a choice to make. I didn't know how to be a mom, but knew I needed to do whatever it took to love and protect this precious child that was being intricately knitted together in my womb. My world was shaken, yet unbeknownst to me, God was working out a good and gracious plan for my life.

In 2004, I made the decision to accept my parents' invitation to live with them again. I dropped the party scene altogether and gave birth to my first baby as a single mom. My mom lovingly sat by my side during my C-section delivery, and together we heard my baby boy's first cry. Witnessing the miracle of life softened my stubborn, selfish heart and allowed me to see the Lord more clearly than ever. I felt God's presence with me, giving me incredible joy and peace despite the circumstances I faced as an unwed mother.

The Lord used this pregnancy and the love for my baby to restore my relationship with Him. He taught me that the deep love I have for my son cannot compare to the immense love He has for me, my son, or any of His children. I learned that nothing can separate us from the love of the Father. A transformation was beginning within me as I decided to surrender and seek after Jesus and choose Him over myself daily.

He began chiseling me, like Michelangelo would a fresh piece of marble: delicately and patiently. (And God will do this for you— He can transform your hardships and weakness into something unimaginably beautiful and strong!)

Zephaniah 3:17 says it beautifully:

> *The Lord your God is with you,*
> *the Mighty Warrior who saves.*
> *He will take great delight in you;*
> *in his love he will no longer rebuke you,*
> *but will rejoice over you with singing.*

Those first three years of my son's life were especially hard in some ways, but at the same time, I was feeling a sense of true contentment that came from relying on Him as my strength. God provided everything my son and I needed, through people donating clothes and toys, a neighbor whom I didn't know before "randomly" giving me their old car (—God's provisions are never really random!), my Grandma leasing us a condo, finding a day care for my son through friends from church, and locating parenting classes for me to attend.

I also experienced the joy of watching my son develop and learn new things. His excitement and enthusiasm for life were contagious. He enjoyed being read to, putting puzzles together, jumping off the side of the pool into my arms, and looking for hermit crabs and shells at the nearby beach. I remember, when he was two years old, how excited he would be to see the moon, repeating its name from his favorite bilingual TV show: "Luna, Mommy! Luna!!" Experiencing his awe drew me in to pause and observe the moon in a way I hadn't before. My son helped me to enjoy the little things in life that I had overlooked before with my overbooked schedule.

I adored spending time taking him outdoors to explore nature through hikes, splashing around in the ocean, catching frogs, and feeding fish at the local fish hatchery. I enjoyed having him help me bake and do art projects. He was like a sponge, quickly and eagerly soaking up everything I taught him.

By four years old he understood addition and subtraction and was reading chapter books on his own. He was my firstborn, and as a single mom giving him my undivided attention, it came naturally to me to want to answer his questions and teach him. I knew he was smart and capable, but I didn't realize it was unique for him to have the level of knowledge he had at four years old. I also didn't see my teaching as homeschooling, but that is, in fact, exactly what I was doing.

When it came time to send my son to kindergarten, homeschooling never crossed my mind. The past four years were wonderful yet incredibly difficult. By this time, I was a newlywed (such a God story! I'll have to share that in another book). I was excited to have the time during the day to meet my new husband for lunch at his college campus, and to pursue interests of mine that had been put on hold.

So, in September of 2009, I happily waved to my son as the yellow bus whisked him off to public school. I went back inside my apartment, sat on the couch, and could actually hear myself breathing. It was THAT quiet! I sat there, enjoying the stillness and feeling relieved that I had made it to this milestone.

Unfortunately, having him in school didn't go as well as I had hoped. Each day my little four-year-old boy spent about an hour on the bus alongside fifth graders who weren't the best influences. He would frequently report happenings on the bus that made my heart sink.

In school, the pressure to conform and fit in began much earlier than I had imagined. This adorable little kindergartner suddenly didn't want me to be picking out his outfits anymore, saying they weren't cool. He developed a sense of self-consciousness that he didn't have before.

Then we found out he had problems with paying attention and being disruptive. He started coming home saying, "I got three flies today." Flies where a cute way of disciplining in the classroom: a child would receive a "fly" as a warning from the teacher—basically, three strikes and you're out. I thought this was a good system at first, until he came home quite regularly with flies. I found it to be ineffective to properly discipline him, since by the time he came home with "three flies," hours had passed since his misbehavior, and I didn't know what needed correction.

After several parent/teacher meetings and analyzing the situation, I came to realize he was bored in class. I certainly don't want to make the mistake of defending bad behavior; he should be taught to be respectful, listen, and follow the rules. However, it made sense to me that my son was not receiving enough stimulation academically and physically, and therefore he was acting out. It didn't help that there was no effective discipline at the moment the behavior problem occurred, either.

As a highly active boy, he needed much more time to run around than the half hour of recess and twice a week PE class he was given. I've read several children's development books that ascertain that boys, in particular, need lots of time to exercise and explore at this age. They learn by doing. I also recognized that, due to the time already invested in teaching him to read and learn, he was not being challenged academically and so was not developing the vitally important skills of problem-solving and working hard. The habit of 'cruising' would later frustrate him when he came upon a difficult problem. I asked about placing him in a gifted program, but gifted and AP courses were not offered until middle school.

Another issue that exposed itself came about when our son started waking up in the middle of the night with nightmares. Before going to school, he had never been afraid of the dark or had trouble with nightmares. I never allowed him to watch or read anything scary. My husband and I approached the teacher about these nightmares after our son told us that "the kitty at school told me there might be skeletons or monsters in my closet." His teacher explained to me that the guidance counselor meets with the class and has a stuffed animal cat she brings with her to help kids talk about their emotions. The kitty would speak to the kids and ask them questions about themselves, while the counselor tried to gauge what the children's home life was like. I found it odd that the counselor would 1) be implanting scary ideas into their heads, and 2) be getting so personal without parental consent.

I now felt uncomfortable with putting my five-year-old son into the care of complete strangers for seven hours of the day, and I missed him. We were becoming more disconnected, and I felt like I was losing him. I wanted to know what he was being taught in addition to academics, and who he was interacting with. I decided visiting him during lunch time was a good way to meet his friends and get a glimpse into what his day was like. My husband also utilized the flexibility of his schedule to visit our son during lunch or volunteer in his classroom.

What we both observed during several lunchtime visits was that the kindergartners all lined up with their trays and were given a complete meal, after which they ate only the dessert and threw the rest away—and there was no one there to monitor what they were eating! I was astounded that these young children were living on a diet of Jello-O, cookies, strawberry milk, and whatever other sweet substance the school provided them.

My husband and I started to seriously question whether public school was a right fit for our son, but still didn't consider homeschooling as an option. I just decided to make it work for the best. I started packing him a lunch every day and would debrief him after school to answer his questions and give him my perspective.

One of the questions he had after school was, "Mommy, a kid in my class said Jesus died a long time ago, and is not alive anymore, but I told him He's alive! Is that right?" I was surprised that, at five years old, he was already encountering opposition to his faith.

The spiritual battle reared its ugly head again in first grade when, in art class, the teacher told the kids to make scary haunted houses, and my son told the teacher he wanted to make a nice house instead. Thankfully, she let him. I praise God for his courage at a young age to go against that, but I felt saddened that his teacher encouraged all the students to do that with their creativity. It was contrary to my family's beliefs, and certainly not what I wanted my child to do with his artistic abilities.

During the month of October, he brought home books from the school library that celebrated Halloween and had pictures of bloody, severed limbs in it. Shocked and appalled, I told him he couldn't check out books like this, and I had to explain why. I felt myself increasingly needing to defend our family's values. It was exhausting to be re-teaching almost daily what was learned through school that I didn't approve of.

The proverbial "straw that broke the camel's back" was when our son came home with a bracelet on his wrist with the words "End the Hate." I asked him where he got it from and he said, "At school. I had to sign a piece of paper, and they gave me this bracelet." I was perplexed. My first grader was asked to sign a paper? For what? What was he agreeing to? The school hadn't contacted the parents about needing to sign any forms. I called the school and found out that an anti-bullying campaign was being promoted in the schools, and the children were shown a video about it.

I wanted to know what he had seen, so I did my own research online. What I found was a video about the "End the Hate" campaign, showcasing incidents of bullying homosexuals, with teens speaking to students about it. I'm not a proponent of ANY bullying, but this was a very mature video for 1st graders. I wish the school would have notified me ahead of time so that I could have had the option to not let him see it, or at the very least to be advised so I could follow up with him about what he saw that was probably very confusing, if not disturbing.

It felt like there was a battle at every turn, and I had no ability to control it. Although my husband and I were involved with the school, we were still unaware of what was going on. I desired more for my son's educational, spiritual, physical, and moral development. I wanted him to be challenged in his reading, and to enjoy books that would motivate him for good, like reading about real-life heroes. I wanted him to have plenty of physical activity and be free to explore the world around him rather than being stuck indoors sitting at a desk for six hours of the day.

I didn't want him to be frightened by spooky ideas planted in his head by the guidance counselor who advised the children to talk to the kitty who would make it all better. No, I wanted to sit next to my son on the couch with a Bible and tell him if he's ever frightened to pray to Jesus—not a fake kitty!

I wanted to be more involved as a parent. Sitting in at lunch wasn't enough to instill our family's biblical values, and I longed for the days when I felt a deep connection to my son. The time we spent together in those preschool days was "filled with wonder and bonding experiences. I relished witnessing his first words, his first steps, his first snowfall. Now, just two years later, I felt detached from him.

I remember calling my mom and expressing my frustration. I wasn't happy with his current situation, and I wanted an alternative. I couldn't afford to send him to private school, and I lacked the confidence to homeschool. (Not only did I think I couldn't do it, I didn't want to lose my precious alone time!)

I asked for her advice, and she gave me counsel that I took to heart. Regarding homeschooling, she said, "You can always try it for a year, and if it doesn't work out, you can send him back to public school." Ahhh—but of course! Why didn't I think of that? It was so freeing to hear that I could try it out and not be locked into this through high school! I already had my husband's support, since he already had a positive experience of being homeschooled for 4 years.

So, after two years of feeling unsettled, we decided to withdraw him from public school and begin homeschooling. I didn't know where to start, or how to do it, but I began talking to people I knew who homeschooled. I learned as I went. What I thought would be impossible not only became possible—it became enjoyable. And nothing can compare to the peace I felt at having my little boy in my care.

Consequently, after successfully making it through the first year, I chose to continue for five more years. Approaching my son's 8th grade year, we had just moved to a new state and wanted to make the transition as easy as possible for him, so my husband and I gave him the option to enter public school. Although my son had enjoyed being homeschooled, he had made new friends in the neighborhood who attended the local public school, so he decided he wanted to give it a try.

Within the first two months of attending public school, my husband and I observed a detrimental decline in some of the content he was learning, his social behaviors, and his own spiritual perspective. And, disturbingly, his safety was at stake. My husband and I sought the Lord on what to do. I didn't want to pull him out mid-year, and I had a hard time making the choice because my son fought me on it. He had just been through a big transition, and I didn't want to cause another one.

God faithfully answered my prayer in a way I could understand clearly. Although it was hard, I acted in faith, following what I believed the Lord was telling me to do. I went to the school office, just before Christmas break, and formally withdrew him. To my surprise, I did not get any backlash from the administration, and my son (who was naturally upset at first) changed his disposition within the first two weeks.

The Lord provided everything I needed for him: a homeschool co-op filled with stimulating classes and social events; Christian friends in like-minded families; an accomplished tutor; and, according to him, an opportunity that was "better than his birthday": TeenPact. TeenPact is a four-day leadership school for homeschooled teens intended to raise up leaders who understand the political process, exhibit responsible citizenship, defend our religious freedoms, and so much more. Begrudgingly, he went—and he came out of it totally hyped up with excitement! (Earning high school credit as a government class was a nice perk, too.) But the best part for me was hearing how spiritually impacting it was for him and how he had made friends who agreed to pray for each other and hold each other accountable. Our son now wants to go again next year as a student leader. This wouldn't have happened had I not obeyed God's calling for me to homeschool again.

☙

Your experiences may not be as dramatic as mine have been, but if this decision is on your mind, then it is just as important for you and your family. This book's purpose is to help walk you through the decision-making process, inform you of the necessary steps, and show you that you CAN homeschool, should you choose to.

Before moving on to the next chapter, take a moment to reflect on the questions below and record your answers. Several chapters have questions or checklists designed to help you articulate your thoughts as you seek God's plan for your family. The notes you make will be the building blocks of your homeschool. (You can email kmcternanwrites@gmail.com to get a free printable version of these lists.) When you have finished reading the book, I encourage you to go back and see what you noted at the end of each chapter. It will be like watching the pieces of a puzzle come together to make a complete picture! Spend some time analyzing your current situation, and list anything that has either prevented you from homeschooling or has discouraged you in the process.

For those currently not homeschooling:

- *Is your desire to be the primary influence on your child?*
- *Do you feel detached from what your child is doing at school?*
- *Do you want to give your child an education from a biblical perspective?*
- *Are you unsettled with your child's current schooling experience? If so, list what you are unhappy with and how you think it could be improved.*
- *Do you feel inadequate to teach your child? If so, why?*

For those currently homeschooling:

- *What made you decide to homeschool initially?*
- *Do you feel you lack vision for your homeschool and need a fresh start?*
- *Are you having a hard time finding balance in your homeschool life?*

Chapter 2

11 Homeschooling Questions Answered

When I seriously started to consider homeschooling, I had many questions about it. I lacked the confidence that I could actually do it, and I needed advice. I also needed to reconcile some negative preconceived notions about it and truly understand what life was like for a homeschooler.

In this chapter, I have answered the most common questions and comments I hear about homeschooling. These honest, matter-of-fact answers are based on my own personal experiences, the experiences of numerous homeschool families, and thorough research. This section will help you to have a clearer idea of what to expect, offer encouragement, and prepare you to answer the "naysayers" you may encounter.

1. If I homeschool, will my child become an unsocialized weirdo, sheltered and unprepared for the real world?

Although most people don't ask this question out loud, this preconceived notion pops into many heads as a serious concern. It's a reasonable thought, since negative media likes to portray homeschoolers as intellectually challenged and overly sheltered, like Harry Dunne from the movie *Dumb and Dumberer* (the prequel to *Dumb and Dumber*).

It seems that most people who do not understand what homeschooling truly is assume that homeschooled children are isolated from society, and therefore are unable to socialize normally and have healthy relationships.

The truth is, many homeschooled children are the most "socialized" individuals you will meet. They are exposed to a wealth of opportunities both in and outside the home that have them interacting with people of multiple ages and stages. One of the things that attracted me the most to homeschooling was the children I met who were homeschooled! They weren't anything like I imagined they'd be.

My cousins, for example, were homeschooled and were the most socially comfortable girls I knew—but I thought they were the exception. Growing up, I admired how they were able to interact with adults so easily, when I would feel awkward and shy around them. These girls were not stuck at home all day. Rather, they were directly involved with their community. They were well known for their friendly service at a nearby farm and for their volunteer efforts with Operation Christmas Child (an organization that ships shoeboxes filled with small gifts to underprivileged children around the world). Every year they helped host a packing party where hundreds of people would attend to donate items and help pack the boxes. One year, they were even featured in the local newspaper for collecting a staggering 4,000 boxes! That's triple the amount my whole church collected!

When I started meeting homeschool families as an adult, I was blown away by the level of maturity the children possessed. I met child after child who profoundly impressed me by their friendly, respectful, and confident demeanor. These kids shone like stars! They showed responsibility, obedience to their parents, poise, gentleness to their siblings, helpful attitudes, and had the ability to carry on intelligent conversations. I found (and still find) the majority of children and adults who were homeschooled to have very attractive personalities.

I believe the majority of parents who homeschool want what is best for their children, and with that comes loving protection. This does not translate to "sheltered." Google's definition for sheltered is "protected from difficulties or unpleasant realities." Antagonists assume that homeschooled children are totally isolated from the outside world, which simply isn't accurate.

Difficulties and hardships arise in our homes, communities, and our world, and from my personal experience, homeschooled children are frequently given a "leg-up" to face such challenges. Why? Because they are often serving in their families and community, learning how to handle various situations.

They also have the time necessary to discuss sensitive topics with their homeschooling parent, and have their heartfelt questions answered in a safe environment. The family bond becomes stronger as parents and children work through trials together.

Likewise, I have found that most of the homeschool curricula available seeks to aid parents in engaging children in thoughtful discussions of various relevant topics. These books not only present subjects from a Christian perspective, but they also describe other worldviews. In the My Father's World curriculum package titled *Exploring Countries and Cultures*, for example, it relates details of other cultures and their religious beliefs.

Another related theory about homeschoolers is that they are not aware of social norms. If "social norm" means embracing the depravity of our culture (such as listening to music or watching movies that glorify violence, drugs, and twisted sexuality), then I'd say yes, most Christian homeschoolers are not exposed to that. This does not mean that the child is unprepared for the world.

The Bible states clearly in Philippians 4:8, "Whatever is true, whatever is noble, whatever is right, whatever is pure, whatever is lovely, whatever is admirable—if anything is excellent or praiseworthy—think about such things." There are ways of discussing issues and unpleasant realities with a child without tainting their innocence.

For example, my family has been supporting our local pregnancy resource clinic for years. This has led to discussions in our home about abortion. I didn't necessarily want my children knowing the painful reality of what abortion entails, but with our service there, we felt it important for them to be aware of this hard truth. We were able to explain it in a way they could comprehend enough to know what it is, while sparing them from graphic pictures and heart-wrenching details of the procedure. We also shared how our family feels about it and what they can do to help. I believe a healthy balance for all children, regardless of where or how they are schooled, is to be aware of what is happening around the world, while having the loving guidance of their parents to be able to discern right from wrong and learn how to take appropriate actions to help society.

The majority of homeschoolers are not unsocialized. On the contrary, they are used to being involved in activities outside their homes and interacting with people in a variety of social contexts. Dr. Brian Ray of the National Home Education Research Institute (NHERI) found, in his research on homeschoolers, that they are "typically above average, on measures of social, emotional, and psychological development." In short, they are well prepared both academically and socially.

2. Do all homeschool moms look homely?

This is a funny question, you might say, but it's a question that honestly went through my mind before I started homeschooling. I was genuinely concerned that I wouldn't fit in with other homeschool moms because I believed a stereotype that homeschool moms are homely, and their children were plain and dorky. ("Dorky"—remember that word? That really reveals my age!) I was actually surprised to see that most of the homeschooling moms I met did not have the image I imagined. What I love about the homeschool community of parents and students is that they are not driven by their appearance. That's not to say they are homely, but rather they are unique individuals from a variety of different backgrounds and education levels. They freely express themselves however they feel comfortable. Some mamas wear long skirts and no makeup. Some mamas fix themselves up in skinny jeans and boots. I do both, depending on the day!

Years later, I have realized that how I look is not as important as how I behave, and I feel thankful to be in a community that accepts me whether I'm in sweats or in heels. We "do community" together with loving respect. I greatly admire this because it's not common in the modern world, especially among women. Ladies can be oh-so-catty! But I have found that the homeschool moms I meet are some of the best people in the world, and their children some of the coolest. May I encourage you not to dismiss getting to know someone based on their appearance? You never know what you can offer that person, or what that person can offer you. She could just be your next BFF!

3. I don't have a college degree. Can I still homeschool successfully?

Absolutely, you can! Studies have proven that homeschool students fare very well, whether or not the parent who taught them was college-educated. According to a recent study by NHERI, "Homeschool students score above average on achievement tests regardless of their parents' level of formal education or their family's household income."[i]

A prime example of how it does not take a college-educated parent to raise a successful college-bound student is the story of Charles Mulli. Mulli was orphaned at a young age and worked incredibly hard to fend for himself, eventually becoming a wealthy businessman. As an adult, he rescued any child he saw who was orphaned and living in extreme poverty as he had been. Together with his wife, Esther, they brought in over 100 children to feed, clothe, bathe, shelter, and teach. Mulli and his wife homeschooled all of them, and they founded an organization—with a slight spelling change—called Mully Children's Family. This charity is now a notable school that has produced doctors, lawyers, and graduates from Ivy League schools like Brown University! This inspiring story was documented in the movie sponsored by Focus on the Family titled *Mully: The World's Largest Family*. Author and theologian C.S. Lewis once said, "The only people who achieve much are those who want knowledge so badly that they seek it while the conditions are still unfavorable."[ii] That is exactly what Mully did, and it's precisely what anyone else can do, should they choose.

The best gift you can give your child is to produce a lifelong love of learning (see chapter 3!). To do this, your child needs to see that YOU are continually learning. Don't pretend to know everything, but don't make yourself out to be a dummy, either! Let your child find you opening up the Word of God for wisdom. Let them walk alongside as you problem-solve when you need an answer. And don't rely solely on Google for information—research through books, too. Your modeling will encourage them to want to open up books to learn from. Your enthusiastic inquisitiveness is important for your child to discover that learning is a lifelong process. It doesn't end after high school or college.

You can be a better home educator through learning along with your children. Just like a muscle that needs exercise to become strong, the more you use your brain, the stronger it gets! "Every time you have a new thought, learn a new word, form a new memory, or learn something, you create more connections in your brain."[iii]

Your brain can never get too full or explode from too much information. Actually, the more you learn, the healthier your brain gets! According to the Amen Clinic, there are many ways you can exercise your brain, and you can do these right along with your children:

- *Brush your teeth with your opposite hand*
- *Word searches*
- *Crossword puzzles*
- *Sudoku*
- *Jigsaw puzzles*
- *Memorize the alphabet backwards*
- *When out walking, try walking backwards for part of the time*
- *Learn to read and play music*
- *Learn to play a new instrument*
- *Learn to speak a foreign language*
- *Online brain games*

Find a supportive homeschool community to connect with where you can share your talents, and where the talents of others can help where you are weak. For example, one of my strengths is planning events, so I have coordinated field trips and fun activities for different homeschool groups we've participated in. My weakness, on the other hand, is math. Through homeschooling I met one of my best friends, who taught math in middle school before having children of her own. When we first chose to homeschool, she introduced us to a math curriculum that worked well for us. Now that my son is past a level I'm comfortable teaching, I have a tutor teach him. We're part of a co-op that offers a wide range of classes like chorus, biology, engineering, physical education, and writing. Being part of a supportive community will enhance your child's experience and will help you in those areas you may not feel confident to teach.

To develop your teaching skills, I recommend the following books: *How Learning Works: Seven Research-Based Principles for Smart Teaching* by Susan A. Ambrose and Michael W. Bridges; *The Core* by Leigh A. Bortins; and *Educating the WholeHearted Child* by Sally Clarkson. As you teach your own children, you'll be amazed by how your own education improves! Learning is a process, and not limited solely to youth. We are all continually growing and taking in new information daily. It's exciting when you and your child discover or learn something together, like watching the circuit you build with your child actually work! Or you can work together to memorize all the names of all the states and capitals for the first time. So, yes—even if you are not college-educated, you are still perfectly capable of teaching your child.

4. Will my child be prepared for college?

Now more than ever, college institutions are recognizing homeschoolers as an asset to their campuses. Education expert Dr. Susan Berry states, "The high achievement level of homeschoolers is readily recognized by recruiters from some of the best colleges in the nation. *Schools such as Massachusetts Institute of Technology, Harvard, Stanford, and Duke University all actively recruit homeschoolers.*"[iv]

Katie Fretwell, Dean of Admission and Financial Aid at Amherst, reported to NBC News regarding homeschoolers: "They tend to have thicker folders, in a good way. They are innovative thinkers with a lot to bring to the table."[v]

Homeschooled children have more focused time to do their studies without the distractions and inhibitions of large classes, and without the time often wasted in a traditional school setting. They generally don't have after-school homework, so they are able to have more time to pursue other interests and develop their individual gifts and talents. Because of this, many excel not only academically but also in extracurricular activities such as music, sports, or STEM areas, allowing them to be key candidates for scholarship money.

Not only that, but homeschoolers often have work experience, giving them valuable skills, and added appeal for recruiters. Most of the homeschoolers I have met complement their academic studies with practical skills, such as on-the-job training outside of the home, starting a business, helping the family business, or having the opportunity to participate in activities that will enhance their education, For example, my son at just 9 years old was involved with Toastmasters, an international organization put together for adults to practice and refine their public speaking skills. This was a unique experience afforded to the homeschoolers in our area. The children would prepare a speech and carry on with the roles given to them, learning to listen and be respectful while others spoke and practicing the skills of a polished presenter.

There are many resources that have inspired me along the way. The book *Homeschooling for Excellence* is one in which the author and his wife, David and Micki Colfax, decided to homeschool their four boys as a result of not being satisfied with the public school system. They gave them a well-rounded, hands-on education, and all of their sons ended up going to Harvard.

Homeschooled children can be fully equipped to excel in college and are statistically at an advantage. "Those who prepare thoroughly can be admitted with full scholarships at those selective colleges that some parents daydream about their children attending," said homeschool dad and educational consultant Karl M. Bunday, who compiled an online list of over 1,000 colleges that have admitted homeschoolers.[vi]

I believe it's also important to note that college is not the only option after completing high school. Some teens will be more suited to a trade school, or they may start their own business. If you recognize that your child is the entrepreneur type, provide ways for them to learn the skills of running a business. If your child is interested in a particular trade, find opportunities for them to apprentice with a trusted and experienced mentor. Not only will your child thrive doing what they are interested in, but they will gain valuable skills for their résumé and future work opportunities.

5. I'm not organized. Can I really homeschool?

I used to feel intimidated by homeschool moms. I saw them as having it all together—you know, super-efficient, ultra-organized, and crazy patient! I believed that all homeschool moms woke up at 5 a.m. to do devotions, bake homemade bread, and milk the cows. (Did I mention I'm definitely NOT a morning person?) I felt inadequate next to these moms who were able to juggle it all effortlessly without losing their cool. I remember attending my first "homeschool parent support group," where a couple who had eight children and had been homeschooling for at least fifteen years was invited to speak. I was in awe at just the introduction of this family! A lady in the group presented them as having a reputation in the community for their kids being incredibly helpful and kind, and the parents seemed so full of joy and peace! I just didn't think I could be like them. I have a past that I was ashamed of (therefore in my mind, NOT the perfect family scenario). I had only one child and he needed serious character training. I wasn't organized, I lacked patience, and, coming from a childhood where almost everything was done for me, I had a difficult time of being a housewife. I could barely plan that night's meal, and I was hearing these homeschool moms speak of what was on their monthly meal plan! I had never heard of meal planning before.

If you feel subpar to the "average homeschool mom," let me assure you that I understand how you feel. It's easy to compare ourselves with others and allow negativity to creep in, convincing us we can't do it. The truth is, though, that YOU CAN DO IT. You can learn to be orderly. You can learn how to teach your children and still have time to get the chores done and have dinner ready when your spouse comes home from work. In the Bible it says, "I can do all things through Christ who strengthens me" (Philippians 4:13). It doesn't say "some things"; it says "ALL things." I truly believe that if you rely on Him, He will make you able, and you will surprise yourself with what you can do! I can say this because I look back on seven years of homeschooling, and I'm amazed by what God has enabled me to do. I'm not saying I have it all together; I recognize my weaknesses, but I have grown exponentially through homeschooling and relying on God's strength in my ability to teach, parent, and run my home.

Also, now that I am a homeschooling mom with many homeschool-mom friends I share life with, I can tell you that everyone has a story. Everyone goes through struggles in their life, and "mom fail" moments where they feel they blew it. Most homeschool moms and dads would share with you that becoming organized and managing the home and children has been a process with great reward. Most were not sure what to teach and have experimented with various curricula and different methods of teaching. These friends of mine will tell you that creating order in their homes and juggling tasks well were all learned experiences. It didn't happen overnight. The many homeschool parents I know didn't have a system in place that worked from the beginning. Rather, they learned as they went, through trial, error, and lots of prayer. And I feel thankful to be able to share with you what I have learned. Later in the book I'll share with you some suggestions for HOW you can have the organized homeschool life you desire.

6. My child is already in public school; does that mean I shouldn't switch?

If you believe your child's current schooling situation is not the best option, don't be afraid to make the bold decision of withdrawing from school. You have been given a great responsibility by God to raise your child to the best of your ability. If God is calling you to homeschool, don't allow anyone's negative input to overshadow that. You can make the decision to homeschool at any time, even in the middle of a school year. (I know because I have done it.) I do believe it would be more difficult of a transition for the child the longer they are in a public school system, but that should not stop you. If your child does not want to be pulled from school, it's important to validate their feelings, but you must do what you believe is right. Youth have many opinions and feelings, but they don't know what is best for them. That's why they have parents to help guide them in life. They will thank you for it later!

7. Can I effectively homeschool the middle- and high-school years?

Absolutely. And no, you won't need to re-learn calculus or quantum physics.

Homeschool curricula such as Abeka, Sonlight, and Alpha Omega are designed to help you instruct through 12th grade, providing DVD or online instruction, answer keys, and teacher support. Sonlight offers an online chat feature on their website to answer any question you have, and membership with the Home School Legal Defense Association (HSLDA) provides you with a high school coordinator you can reach by email or phone.

There are also many community groups that provide classes and social activities, such as prom, for youth. Classical Conversations has a complete curriculum for high school students, with instructional days once a week in a classroom setting. Other options like correspondence and cover schools offer a variety of high school classes, as well as testing, grading, four-year high school planning, transcripts, and diplomas. (See the resource section at the back of the book for listings on these.) HSLDA and Liberty University both issue diplomas to homeschoolers and host traditional graduation ceremonies. There are also many people who dedicate time to teach homeschooled students, such as retired science teachers and engineering professors.

In my own family, my mom decided to homeschool my brother in middle school, when the school administrators where insisting that she put him on Ritalin to help him focus. Ritalin is a serious, habit-forming drug used to calm children down so they aren't hyperactive. My mom knew that solution was wrong for him. With him at home, she was able to observe that he only had trouble focusing when given a task he didn't want to do. When given the liberty to read a technical manual like instructions to his paintball gun, he was absorbed! He thrived in a distraction-free environment where he could pursue his interests, like taking apart a radio and putting it back together. He's now a mechanical engineer.

My husband was pulled out of public school and homeschooled during his middle school years, as well. He claims confidently that they were the best school years of his life. He attributes his love of science and what he does today (rocket science) to his mom who taught him, and sparked excitement in him for learning. Please read his words in the Foreword.

So, rest assured, homeschooling can be done at any point. Don't be discouraged if you feel you've missed the homeschool bandwagon because your child is already in public school. If you feel a desire to homeschool, with diligence and God's help, you can do it.

8. Should I homeschool when my family won't support my decision?

One of the most important things to consider when you begin homeschooling is who your support will be. Fortunately for me, my husband, in-laws, and my parents were supportive of my decision to homeschool. I have had many friends who have "gone against the tide" and decided to homeschool even though their parents or in-laws or friends didn't agree with it. Some of them have shared their stories in the Testimonials section of the book for you to read.

Although it is possible to homeschool without your parents' or friends' support, I wouldn't advise making this decision without your spouse's support. If the Lord is calling you to do it, but your spouse is not on board, pray that God will speak to him/her also. It's truly important that you're in agreement, and for your child to see you're on the same page.

Now, if you're a single mom or dad and think there's no hope for doing this, think again! I also have friends who are single that have successfully homeschooled their child/children. Again, you can find some of those stories at the end of the book that will serve as encouragement to you.

Although I had the backing of my family, I lived far from them and needed to find a supportive community. Having people to interact with that understood both the joys and struggles of homeschooling was life-giving to me. The community I had gave me advice, shared education materials, carpooled with me, brought over meals when I was healing from my C-sections, celebrated together my new babies and birthdays, went on field trips and homeschool conferences, offered unique skills to share with my children, and so much more. Whether you have the support of your family or not, it is imperative that you find a solid homeschool community for both you and your children.

9. Must I be a morning person to homeschool?

As I implied earlier in this chapter, I have never been a morning person. Growing up, I remember my mom teasing me saying, "The early bird gets the worm!" And as a teen I sarcastically retorted, "Yeah, but the second mouse gets the cheese." Before having children, it was a miracle if I was up before 9 a.m. I'd feel sluggish in the morning, but I'd perk up around 10 o'clock at night. I was a night owl, just like my dad. My firstborn did not take after me this way; he was up at 5 a.m. consistently for about the first five years of his life, and oh-so-peppy!! I remember dragging myself out of bed with my eyes like little slits as I sauntered down the stairs to the living room with my energetic, let's-greet-the-day child!

That early riser of mine is now a teenager and learning the skill of sleeping in (!), while I have now become accustomed to getting up early, sometimes before my children. I have found that if I'm up and ready before them, I have a better handle of the day itself. *Rise and Shine Recipes and Routines for Your Morning,* by Megan Schreiber, is filled with wisdom from a seasoned homeschool mom of six and has inspired my morning routine.

My morning schedule has changed quite a bit year to year, depending on our life circumstances. Now that my youngest is sleeping through the night, I feel more capable to have a morning routine, but this didn't happen overnight (no pun intended!).

If you are up at night with a baby, it's hard to have a morning routine. One of the nice things about homeschooling is you are free from rushing around in the morning to get your child ready and on the bus by 7 a.m. I remember how stressful that was for me, back when I was recovering from a C-section and up every 2-3 hours at night. After having "one of those nights," you'll appreciate the benefit of sleeping in until your kids wake you up.

If it's an option, ask your spouse to take the morning "shift." After my husband read *The Miracle Morning* by Hal Enrod, it inspired him to wake up earlier, drink a glass of water, and include our boys in an exercise routine before going to work. He also helps them get dressed, unstack the dishwasher, make breakfast, and say the Pledge of Allegiance outside our front door. (As a side note, we moved into our home a few months ago, and it makes me wonder what our new neighbors think about this processional outside our front door each morning, with my husband and our boys standing with hands on their hearts looking up at the flag!)

The time my husband gives me in the morning helps me tremendously to get the day started on the right foot. I can take care of the baby's needs, read my Bible, pray, and get myself ready before my sons start school.

So, the short answer to this question is, no, you do not have to be a morning person in order to homeschool your children. However, it's important to remember we are all given the same 24 hours a day to work with, and you want to be as productive as possible. What time you begin school in your home is up to you. That's part of the wonderful flexibility homeschooling affords, though I definitely recommend coming up with a schedule you can work from and sticking to it as much as possible.

10. What do I do when I lose patience with my child and feel like giving up?

As much as you love your sweet blessing of a child, that child has their moments where they will drive you crazy, and I will not judge you for wanting to hide in your bathroom with the door locked! While you may think you need to have the patience of a saint to homeschool, I can tell you that this mama has had to apologize to my children for yelling at them—and I have certainly had days where I felt like sending them on that big yellow bus.

The key here is this: know that it is completely normal to have days where you will want to give up. That's not to discourage you, but for you to expect it, because if you go into homeschooling expecting your children to now be sweet little angels (when, instead, they can't be quiet for five minutes during a read-aloud), you will only get frustrated and disappointed. Character training takes time and effort. You will see results, but they don't happen as quickly as we'd like. Children need continual discipleship and discipline.

Also, know that the enemy will not be happy with you discipling your child in the ways of the Lord; he will do everything he can to stop you. Often, this comes in the form of doubt: doubting your parenting skills; doubting whether you made the right decision; doubting that you can homeschool, period. Hold those defeating thoughts captive! Don't let them play out in your mind; pray against them.

I highly recommend you put yourself in "time-out" if you need to. Take a five- to ten-minute breather in your room or the bathroom with the door locked. You can even tell your child you need a time-out to think and relax so you won't say something you shouldn't. It will help you keep calm. During your "break," call up a trusted friend or support partner who will understand what you're going through and can listen to your frustrations. I have a few good friends I communicate with when the going gets rough. At times we'll text asking for prayer when we need it, and texts come back with encouraging words and verses from Scripture. It really helps to have that support and to know you're not alone in this.

Another thing you can do, once you've had time to "take a breather," is to try something else. Are you losing patience because your child isn't understanding a mathematical concept? Or is it that your sons keep bickering with each other? In either situation, your response could change everything. With the math example, you could try explaining it a different way, e.g. in a way that would be applicable to a real-life scenario. ("If we go to the store, and you have $25 to buy your favorite toy, and it costs $21 . . .") In the other example, it's losing patience over what seems a never-ending battle. Again, try something different. Try separating them; maybe they need their individual space, especially if you have an introverted child paired with an extrovert. Recognize that the introvert will need some alone time during the day to be in their own head to problem-solve, think, and create.

Proverbs 31:26 says, "She opens her mouth with wisdom, and the teaching of kindness is on her tongue." (ESV) As moms and educators, we cannot reach our children if we're treating our kids harshly. As soon as you feel impatience bubbling up inside of you, walk into another room, take a deep breath, pray, and don't speak to your child until you have the self-control to speak kindly. As you practice this, you'll break the habit of reactionary parenting. If you have a child that is defiant by nature, this is particularly vital for you, as you need to exercise patience more than with the average child. A strong-willed child likes to argue, and they may enjoy getting a reaction from you, even if it's negative. Something that has greatly helped me to stay calm and my son to argue less is setting up a chart. Together with my husband, we sat down with our son and asked him what he thought would be fair consequences for certain behaviors. Then, we wrote them down once they were all agreed upon. During the day, if one of those negative behaviors emerged, I would go to the chart and patiently point out what we had agreed to. It's amazing how my son responded so well to it; he couldn't argue with the punishment because he was involved in the process of deciding the consequences. If you can be self-controlled and unwavering in your discipline, you will teach your child that their negative behavior can't cause you to back down or give in to them.

11. I'm a single parent. Is it possible for me to homeschool?

If you're a single parent that wants to homeschool, let me assure you that you are not excluded from being able to do it well. It's completely normal to doubt yourself, but studies have proven that homeschooled children perform well regardless of living in a single-parent or dual-parent environment. Dr. Brian D. Ray of NHERI states, "When a child is home-educated, the child does as well academically, socially, emotionally and psychologically as other students. Study after study shows that home schoolers outperform those in public school and [do] at least as well as private school students. This fact remains the same for single-parent and two-parent families."

I remember when I was a young, unmarried college student faced with an unplanned pregnancy, thinking, "How am I going to do this?" Yet, somehow you manage, right? And you try your hardest because you want what is best for your child. With homeschooling, it's much the same. Doubting your ability is normal—and, yes, it will be a challenge at first—but if you truly want to homeschool, you'll find ways to make it happen. I'll help you to figure out how.

One of your biggest concerns may be financial support for your family while homeschooling. In order to provide for your children, you need to work, and your job may be what is preventing you from homeschooling. There are several options you might consider:

- *You can school around your work schedule. Homeschooling offers you the flexibility to school around your schedule. You can teach after work, before work, and on weekends.*
- *If your child is old enough, they can participate in an online school while you're at work.*
- *You can find a job with better hours or look for a work-from-home position.*
- *Some homeschool co-ops offer drop-off classes. Look for these in your area.*

There are many resources available to help homeschoolers in financial need, such as the Homeschool Foundation. Their mission is "helping homeschool families in hard times." Latasha was one such recipient of their help. She lost her husband to lung cancer, and without her family's support she struggled to provide on her limited income. The Homeschool Foundation gave her a grant, with which she was able to purchase the books, electronics, and materials she needed for homeschooling. Of this gift she says, "What a blessing! This grant will help him take baby steps in his dream [of being a doctor] and lead him to bigger things. Every time my son says, 'Thank you, Mom, for homeschooling me,' it literally brings me to tears. Losing my husband has not been easy, but the Lord gave us the strength to carry on."[vii]

If cost is a factor, there are also several options for free or low-cost curriculum. Ambleside Online (amblesideonline.org) and Easy Peasy All-In-One Homeschool (allinonehomeschool.com) both provide homeschoolers with well-rounded, thoroughly-planned-out lessons that are completely free. You can also seek out homeschool publishers, as some offer payment options. Many of them list their phone numbers or chat boxes on their websites, encouraging people to ask them questions. Alpha Omega and Sonlight are just two examples of this. You can find more in the Resources section.

If you don't have a support system in place already, make sure that you find one. Having the support of friends, family, church family, or other homeschool parents will be important to your emotional well-being. They can encourage you, pray with you, assist with childcare, rides, and teaching or mentoring. For online support and encouragement geared toward the single parent, you can visit heartofmichelle.com. This blog is written by a single mom of 5 who homeschools. She has experience raising children with dyslexia and bipolar disorder and offers advice and support on those topics also. More encouragement for the single parent can be found at notconsumed.com, which is run by Kim Sorgius, single homeschool mom of four. She also wrote a book titled *Single Mom Homeschooling* which may be a great resource for you.

If your child's biological parent is involved in your child's life, they may not want you to homeschool. If you have sole custody, you are able to make that decision regardless, but it is still wise to present the matter in a way they will be more receptive to. Feel free to show them the benefits that are listed in this book. Additionally, consider whether they would be able to help teach a subject or life skill, or to contribute to paying for a tutor. If that is not possible, don't feel discouraged. Seek counsel from those who have been where you have, whether a trusted friend, counselor, or through a homeschool group. This will greatly help to give you the support you need. If you have any legal questions regarding homeschooling as a single parent, contact the Home School Legal Defense Association.

I was inspired by the story of Ben Carson. While he was not formally homeschooled, his single mother, who worked 2-3 jobs to provide for her sons, taught Ben and his brother when they came home from school. She could barely read herself, but she made them read two books a week and write a report on each. She had them problem-solve and work hard. Today, Dr. Carson is among the world's best neurosurgeons, and he is famous for successfully separating conjoined twins who were joined at the back of the head, among many other amazing medical accomplishments. At the time of this writing, Dr. Carson holds a cabinet position under President Donald Trump as the US Secretary of Housing and Urban Development. In an interview with HSLDA, Dr. Carson stated, "*We know that the very best education is homeschool.*"[viii]

Homeschooling without a partner isn't easy, but once you get into a working routine you'll grow more confident. Be at peace knowing that God will provide for you and give you the strength you need to teach your children. In the Testimonials section, you'll be encouraged by two homeschooling single moms who have shared why they made this choice, along with helpful advice on how it works for them.

❦

Hopefully, after reading this chapter, some of your biggest concerns have been addressed, and you feel more confident in making a decision that is right for your family. Take note of anything from this chapter that spoke to you, pray about it, and get ready to be impressed—the next chapter will highlight many of the amazing homeschool benefits!

Chapter 3

Bountiful Benefits

There is a plethora of benefits to homeschooling. When I first started, I had no idea just how many advantages would result from it. An immediate benefit for me was to be the primary influence over my son, but it has proven to be so much more.

It Will Benefit YOU!

The most surprising benefit to homeschooling was the positive changes it had on me personally. I considered all the benefits for my child, but I never expected it to benefit ME. Through homeschooling my children, I have experienced growth in my relationship with the Lord, within my own character, in my parenting, and growth in the way I manage my household. I've experienced exciting new adventures with my family, rediscovered lost passions of mine, connected with my children on a deeper level, and have gained much more knowledge.

Homeschooling also gave me the opportunity to develop solid friendships with those of like mind, whose children were being taught similar values. It has been a blessing doing life together with families who share similar joys and struggles.

Flexibility

One of my favorite things about homeschooling is the flexibility. For me, flexibility equals freedom. When my son was in public school, I was frustrated with how much our schedule was dictated by the school calendar. My sister's wedding was in September one year, and we needed enough time to fly there and back and visit with family whom we hadn't seen in ages. If I homeschooled, I could bring the lessons with me on the plane, for example, but with public school he would miss instruction time and need special permission to go. If the absence was considered unexcused, he may use up all his sick days, so that if he did get sick later on in the semester, he would either be forced to go to school sick or be considered "truant." Each state has their own truancy laws, but basically if a child is truant, the family could be called into court, and the child might not be allowed to progress to the next grade level.

With homeschooling, you can decide what your child's schedule will be. Every child is required to attend school for a certain amount of days or hours, as determined by the state, whether in public, private, or homeschool. The difference is those requirements can be in your time. You choose when to start your schooling day and when you will take breaks. If there's a fresh snowfall in the morning and your kids are eager to get outside in it, you have the freedom to start school with building a snow fort and sledding. If your child is sick with an illness easily treated at home, you have the freedom to stay home rather than dragging them to the doctor just to prove your child is ill. Instead, they can rest while doing something educational, such as listening to an audiobook. Or, they can take the day off without risking an "unexcused absence" or miss out on valuable teaching time that could leave them behind.

If you want to plan a family vacation during the school year, you can do so! I personally love being able to schedule family holidays during off-peak season when there are fewer crowds and lower prices. I also appreciate doing school on some of the off days for public school, such as an occasional Saturday or on a 'snow day', so that we can be finished with the mandatory school days before public school gets out for summer. Typically, our school year ends in early May.

You can also decide who will teach. Will it be you, your spouse, or a tutor? Or a combination, perhaps? I have a friend who has a doctorate in biology, and her husband has a doctorate in mathematics. She does the majority of the homeschooling, but her husband teaches their sons math, and they outsource their English lessons to an online instructor.

In our home, I am the primary teacher, but my husband will often teach valuable life skills such as how to change a tire, use a fire extinguisher, mow the lawn, and balance a budget. When my husband was Professor of Engineering Design at Penn State

University, he included our oldest son (who was in 7th grade at the time) in his classroom to supplement his education at home.

You also have the freedom to decide WHAT to teach your child. There are required subjects that need to be taught according to the law, but you are able to decide what books your child will learn from. With well over one million homeschoolers—and growing!—in the US today, there are an abundance of homeschool curricula and materials to choose from. Just visit any homeschool conference and you will be amazed (and possibly overwhelmed) by all of your choices. As a Christian, I wanted to include Bible lessons and texts that taught from a biblical perspective. It was also important for me to choose reading material that would help build godly character, such as heroic tales of notable men and women of history.

Besides the core courses, you'll want to enhance your child's education with subjects that will bring out their natural talents and interests. For example, my 2nd grader loves to draw and paint. In a classroom setting, where there are multiple children to teach and only a certain amount of time given, he would feel rushed and distracted. It's frustrating for an artist to have their creativity interrupted! Yet at home, he has the time necessary to focus while honing his skill and completing a beautiful painting in a day or two. One of his current favorite lessons is following along with a Bob Ross instructional video we found on Amazon Prime.

Lively Texts!

When I made the decision to homeschool, I was given some used books that my aunt had used to homeschool her girls. I was totally blown away by what I saw—never before had I read such lively textbooks. These Christian homeschool texts explained the subjects through engaging stories, in a way children could relate to, while clearly stating the facts. I found them fascinating, and it produced a desire in me to want to learn more. I wondered why core curriculum textbooks weren't more like these. The textbooks I read in school were dull in comparison.

In some ways you could say I received a "swiss cheese" education growing up. I went to several different schools, both public and private, and most of them took God out of the picture. I didn't realize there were holes in my education until reading several of my son's homeschool books. I was fascinated by the story of Pocahontas, for example. I had learned in school about how she saved an Englishman from her father's fierce execution, but never heard how she became a Christian because of the English settler John Rolfe, whom she later married. This beautiful part of the story was missing from the public school textbook. In Apologia's Astronomy textbook written by Jeannie Fulbright, I learned all sorts of amazing facts, such as how God designed birds to follow the constellations in the sky like a giant map when migrating! I felt I was filling in the gaps of my own education as I read these books along with my child. Even if you attended a private Christian school, I'm sure that you, too, will learn so much, as you are being

45

immersed in the education, reading alongside your child, and sharing in the experience of growth.

My son gobbled these books up! They produced in him a desire to read and learn because of how engaging they were. The second year of homeschooling, we chose our own curriculum at a homeschool convention and had them shipped to our house. The day those books arrived at our doorstep was one to remember. My son couldn't wait to unpack the massive package of new materials, and immediately started to read the books, even though it wasn't a school day. I was thrilled that he enjoyed absorbing these texts as much as I did.

Your Classroom is the World

Take advantage of the freedom you have to incorporate lessons beyond the desk. Desks are useful, and I would make sure that your child does have a proper place to sit and do their work. However, it is not necessary to sit at a desk for the entire length of the school day. Instead, as you decide, your child can take their sketchbook outside on a nice day, read English literature lessons in a hammock, bounce on a yoga ball during a history lesson, cuddle with you on the couch for a read-aloud, or write a research paper at the local library.

Homeschool classes are offered by local co-ops, national parks, museums, and even amusement parks—really! Hersheypark in Hershey, Pennsylvania, offers special discounts and classes to homeschoolers. Once a year they host a Physics Day where hersheypark.com says students can "apply the principles of physics to measure how force, energy, mass, and other concepts keep *Hersheypark* rides going up . . . and coming down!"[ix]

Some homeschool families choose to take their children on mission trips during the school year, visit other states for field trips, or literally use the world as their classroom to study languages and culture. Robin Lee Graham was one such individual. Homeschooled and trained in seamanship, shipboard maintenance, and navigation, he set sail around the world at age sixteen, making him the youngest person to sail solo around the world. As you can imagine, no classroom could ever compare to instilling the skills, knowledge, and self-confidence Robin obtained from that experience. While you may not be one to sail around the world with your child, educational trips can develop your child's problem-solving and relational skills, and your family will have meaningful bonding time. For ideas on educational trips and homeschool family excursions, see the list of resources at the end of the book.

You Are the Primary Influence

It has been extremely refreshing to be proactive with the choices I made for my child, rather than reacting to an unfortunate scenario. When my son was in public school I would often get caught in a stressful situation I wasn't prepared for. Take the video about bullying gay students that I mentioned before. It forced me to have conversations that I didn't believe my kindergartner was ready for.

In schools all across America today, teachers are being required to tell children as young as five that they can choose their sexual orientation! I can't imagine my little boy being told that he can be a girl if he wants to. Can you imagine the confusion of these little ones, and how God's heart must ache? I would much rather address topics like sexuality with my child first, *before* the opinion or presentation from someone else, especially when their ideology differs drastically than mine (whether that be a child or teacher).

While your child is young and impressionable, you will want to decide who your child spends most of their time with. With homeschooling, you are able to know who your child is interacting with and can guide those relationships. Just as a brother and sister who quarrel and sometimes need the loving guidance of a parent to step in and help them figure things out, so it is important for a young child to receive helpful instruction with their peers as well. Your child will gain valuable life skills and will feel protected when you step in to help direct a difficult scenario. Typically, in homeschooling circles, you're surrounded by people who have a common goal, and the community helps navigate the children towards that goal. For example, in the Classical Conversations community, their motto is "to know God and make Him known." The families in it are doing their best to live their lives to honor God and to share the good news with others. It is a blessing to be part of a group that shares the same value set as you do, and who can help you raise your children in a way that you so desire.

There are many homeschool activities and groups to choose from. Find one that has similar goals as you do for your child, and together you'll have the benefit of making friends with like-minded people.

An Individualized Education Suited to Each Child

No two children are alike, even within the same household. Any parent of more than one child will recognize this. I was amazed to see the differences between my firstborn and second-born, even as babies. My firstborn emerged into the world with a bang! As a baby he displayed charisma, intellect, and a ton of energy (dropping his naps at age 2). He was often called "precocious," as he was able to speak in small sentences at the age of 1, and he could read fluently by age 4. As a youngster, he used his communication skills to tell people about Jesus on the playground, make people laugh, and debate his cause. As a teen, he continues to read advanced texts, make people laugh, and doesn't shy away from public speaking opportunities such as when he presented a bill before a mock legislature at the Georgia state capitol.

My second-born amazed us early on with his musical abilities and calm demeanor. As a toddler, he would carefully sound out songs he'd hear on the piano. I can still hear his precious 2-year-old voice blaring out, "Re-joice! Re-joice! E-mma---nuel," as he played the piano. He also made up his own songs while strumming a guitar-shaped puzzle piece! (Eventually we bought him a ukulele to strum!) At seven years old, he produces beautiful artwork, continues to enjoy playing music, and his patient, caring attitude is a joy to our family and others.

Nothing compares to an education that is personalized to each child, and with homeschooling that is exactly what your child will be able to receive. An individualized education means they can be taught at their level, pace, learning style, and with their unique interests and talents in mind.

In a large-group educational setting, the teacher has no choice but to teach the whole class at one level and advance accordingly. In this type of environment, there will be children who need more time to understand the material, those that do fine, and those who need to progress but are held back until the rest of the class is ready. When you teach at home, you can move ahead in the lesson when your child is ready, or slow down until the child understands the lesson fully before moving on. This type of learning environment prevents academic frustration, laziness, and boredom. It allows the child to be continually motivated and challenged.

With homeschooling, your child isn't confined to books by grade level. Your child may be the age of a 2nd grader, learning English at a 4th grade level, while needing a 1st grade math book. That can be done with homeschooling.

Another huge benefit to an individualized education is that your child will be able to ask questions and have them answered promptly without feeling stupid, shy, or slowing down the classroom time. With any large class size, it would be virtually impossible to answer every child's questions. Instead, those questions need to be reserved for after class, tutoring, or for the parents once the child gets home from school (and by this time the question is usually forgotten, or the child is too tired at the end of the day to want to learn).

Your child isn't bound to the typical lecture/listen format, either. With homeschooling, you are able to teach with your child's particular learning style in mind. There are four main types of learning styles: visual, auditory, read/write learning, and kinesthetic. With young children, presenting them with all four types helps you to discover how your child learns best. Once you discover that, you can use their learning style to teach them in a way that will help them best comprehend and retain the information being taught, while keeping them interested. For example, if your child is a kinesthetic learner, you will need to provide ways for them to be hands-on. They may not as readily understand how to add by watching you write 2 + 2 = 4 as they would by having four apples to manipulate, for example. You can show them that when you put two green apples together with two red apples, you get four apples all together.

An individualized education also means your child will have more time to foster the talents that God has given them (no waiting for the class, lessons are finished earlier, no homework, etc.). This is arguably the most fun for the child and exciting for you, as you are privy to seeing the unique gifts of your child grow and develop. No matter what education you give your child, you can develop their talents, but with homeschooling it is even easier to recognize your child's abilities because you have a greater amount of time to observe and interact with your child.

Bethany Hamilton, the award-winning surfer, was homeschooled after 6th grade when her parents noticed the undeniable talent she had and wanted her to have more time to pursue her love and talent of surfing. Her parents instilled Bible knowledge and moral character and allowed her time to develop this incredible gift which has led to her traveling the world as a professional surfer, speaker, mentor, and author. She even had a movie made after her called *Soul Surfer,* and she has developed her own charitable foundation to help support amputees and shark attack survivors like herself called Friends of Bethany.

Minimal Distractions and Less Stress

Homeschooling provides a focused learning environment. There are minimal distractions compared to a school setting. Sure, you may have a crying baby or a younger sibling vying for attention, but these are minimal in comparison. Your homeschooled child does not have the pressures like they would in a school environment that would interrupt their learning, and therefore they are able to use the most brain capacity for their studies. They are also at peace in a place where they are accepted and loved.

Of all the things I remember most about my education in public school, it wasn't the distributive law, or the contents of *1984* by George Orwell; it was all the social aspects. I can clearly recall details such as who liked who, being chased by a boy trying to kiss me in 6th grade, my first (awkward!) dance in 8th grade, or who got picked as "most popular" for yearbook. Unfortunately, I have only a vague recollection of most of my academics, even the lessons I studied for months, like how blood travels through the heart or the time I invested in Milton's epic *Paradise Lost,* dissecting it line by line.

My point is this: the social aspect of school, for someone as social and prone to distraction as I, prevented me from absorbing the material being taught. This is the case for many children. Now we have a label for it: ADHD. This is a known brain dysfunction, but I also believe it is over-diagnosed and not given much practical thought. If you think about it, in a classroom of the average thirty students, most would be affected by those around them, whether they are considered a "social" child or not.

This impedes learning in a number of ways. The brain is not able to concentrate on the one thing that matters: learning. It is split into processing not just the lesson being taught, but other factors like the atmosphere of the class, how others perceive them, if the teacher will be pleased with them or not, the interactions that took place before class, or the nerves associated with giving a presentation in the next class.

The students today are faced with even more diversions than I had as a child. Presently, children and youth have to deal with comparing themselves to their peers on a whole new level—internet and texting. Cell phones, tablets, and other media devices are sometimes allowed in class, and almost always allowed during recess. Most of the phones are smartphones, and even if the school has restricted internet, many kids find their way around that using their provider's cell service, not the school's WIFI. Students are actively following friends on social media sites like SnapChat and Instagram which adds to a student's inability to concentrate at school.

It's hard to imagine kids as being stressed out, but statistics are showing that more adolescents are facing depression and anxiety than ever before. According to the Department of Health and

Human Services, more than three million adolescents aged 12 to 17 reported at least one major depressive episode in 2017, and more than two million reported severe depression that impeded their daily functioning.

Ellen Chance, co-president of the Palm Beach School Counselor Association, says that, in her area, "Anxiety and depression are affecting kids' behavior and their ability to learn, which can lead to dropping out or home school." She also reports seeing evidence that technology and online bullying are affecting kids' mental health as young as 5th grade, particularly girls.[x] "I couldn't tell you how many students are being malicious to each other over Instagram," she says. "I've had cases where girls don't come to school and they are cutting themselves and becoming severely depressed because they feel outcasted and targeted." Tragically, she says she now sees cutting incidents pretty much weekly at her elementary school.

Another interruption of effective learning is that of badly-behaved kids in the classroom. A disrespectful student causes disruption to those around them and ends up wasting valuable teaching time. If the teacher does not know how to discipline, or is not empowered to carry out proper consequences, then the disruptive student gets away with their detrimental actions and the whole class suffers. Most American public schools denote increasing lack of respect from students to those in authority and many instances of poorly-behaved students not receiving effective consequences. Often these youth are given warnings (which are not necessarily effective), detention (which is often social time with their peers, again, not always effective), and their parents are notified (who typically don't know what to do since they did not see what took place and may be manipulated by the child). There just isn't the time or the proper authority to discipline well, and we are living in a time where morality is relative—there are no absolutes—so training in godly character is like an endangered species.

Homeschooled children also need training in right living, and while at home they are able to be disciplined immediately following a poor choice. They can learn what the Bible says about a particular offense (such as lying) without peer embarrassment. They have the privilege of having you as their teacher *and* parent: a wonderfully effective, God-given combination of authority to teach, train, and take disciplinary action in love.

Health and Safety

No one will love your child like you do. You are your child's best advocate and protector, and home is where a child should be loved and shielded. Love helps nurture a child to learn and grow into a healthy, stable person. It is because of the love you have for your child that you desire they succeed in life, and you'll put in the effort to give them the best. This includes our sons' and daughters' overall health and safety.

We all know when Mama Bear strikes, it isn't pretty! If you knew your child was being bullied on the playground or was about to be shown an explicit text message, you would step in right away to defend your baby. In a school setting, a bullied child often goes unnoticed or undefended. A major problem in schools now is cyber-bullying and digital abuse. While homeschoolers aren't free from this type of abuse, it is FAR less likely since you can monitor how they use the Internet and help guide the type of friends they hang out with.

The emotional harm that can come to a child through bullying and emotional abuse has devastating effects and should not be ignored. Yet many children who are suffering from a bully often don't have the confidence to tell their parents or a trusted mentor. They try to deal with it, and don't stand up to it because they lack the self-confidence to do so.

The child taught at home is more likely to be protected from the emotional and physical abuse of bullies, as well as other forms of harmful exposures. In school, your child is one of the masses. While school administrators care about the students' safety, they are not able to accommodate, mentor, or protect each child individually. Schools should be a safe haven for children, educators, and school officials themselves, but schools in America today are facing serious safety concerns.

All across America schools are finding it necessary to pay for police officers to guard the school, have metal detectors installed, and make sure their doors are locked during school hours. It's distressing that included in the CDC's school preparation list, they advise that "safety should also be on everyone's back-to-school list."[xi] Among the safety issues the CDC listed to prepare for are bullying, threats with weapons, sexual violence, and suicide. In addition to fire drills or tornado drills, students are now required to have active shooter response training.

Another high area of concern within America's public schools is the nationwide drug epidemic that is killing our teens. It is so serious that, in August of 2017, President Trump declared it "a national emergency. We're going to spend a lot of time, a lot of effort and a lot of money on the opioid crisis." According to the Center for Disease Control, the death rate of teenagers overdosing on drugs "has more than doubled since 1999. In 2015 alone, there were 772 drug overdose deaths for adolescents ages 15 through 19."[xii]

The current statistics on crime and safety in our public schools are alarming. In the joint publication supported by the federal government from the Bureau of Justice (BJS) and the National Center for Education Statistics (NCES) titled *Indicators of School Crime and Safety*, it is reported, "During the 2013–14 school year, 65 percent of public schools recorded that one or more incidents of violence had taken place, amounting to an estimated 757,000 crimes. During the 2014–15 school year, there were 1.3 million reported discipline incidents in the United States for reasons related to alcohol, illicit drugs, violence, or weapons possession that resulted in a student being removed from the education setting for at least an entire school day. About 78 percent of these discipline incidents were violent incidents."

In addition to problems of drugs, violence, and crime in public schools is sexual abuse, most often stemming from children and youth having access to explicit content through their wireless devices. The Associated Press and MTV conducted a survey in 2011 that showed more than half of the respondents claimed they have been victims of harassment on social media or text messages.[xiii] In this study, 76 percent of 14- to 24-year-olds say digital abuse is a serious problem for people their age, with 56 percent reporting that they have experienced abuse through social and digital media. According to an article by Great Schools, sexting is a common problem in schools today with serious consequences. In the article, there are specific examples of youth who have been harshly bullied and abused in school as a result of sexting, which in some cases resulted in suicide. Jessica Logan was one of those examples. She was harshly bullied after her explicit photo circulated around her school. Classmates tormented her by calling her vicious names and throwing harmful objects at her. Her parents filed a lawsuit against her school, claiming administrators didn't do enough to stop classmates from harassing her.

It is not my desire to put fear in your heart, but to alert you to the staggering reality that faces us right now. Fear should never be a driving force compelling you to do anything, so I am not suggesting that you should homeschool your child based on being afraid to send them to school. However, we should not blindly send our children to school, thinking, "if I made it through ok, they will." We need to be proactive with our children's education and safety and seek the Lord's will for each of our children.

God's Word says, "Trust in the Lord with all your heart and lean not on your own understanding. In ALL your ways, acknowledge Him and He will direct your paths." (Proverbs 3:5-6)

The Lord will direct you to know what to do. He will protect your child if it's meant to be that they go to public school.

My parents acted in faith when they sent me to boarding school for my 11th and 12th grades. God made it clear to them to send me to a school in England, and they acted in faith even though they weren't sure why or how they would do it. God blessed that obedient decision in numerous ways. Going into that school, I was a rebellious teen with no faith in God. I heard passing stories from other students about drug use, sexual activity, sneaking out, and alcoholism, but God protected me from all that. He divinely placed me in a room with two missionary kids. It was through these sweet, godly roommates that I became saved. Those two years were the best schooling years of all the countries I lived in and the schools I attended. I'm thankful my parents took the time to listen to the Lord's plan for me and act in faith, even though they couldn't see what the outcome would be.

Biblical Character and Habit Training

Christian home education is not just about academics. It is about instilling biblical lessons, character development, and good habits.

With any person, positive character training can only come about through the working of the Holy Spirit. The overflow of that is peace, love, joy, patience, kindness, goodness, gentleness, faithfulness, and self-control. If you take the Bible out of the picture, the base, raw, animal-like human nature takes over. You'll have problems like selfishness, pride, and deceitfulness. Teaching from the Bible can penetrate the heart, effectively teaching appropriate behavior and instilling moral character. If your child is struggling with self-control, you can do exercises during the day that will teach them to be self-controlled, and have the child memorize scripture relating to that character quality.

You will have the ability to admonish the child when you see them making the choice to fight with their siblings, lie, or talk back. A child that is lovingly discipled and disciplined will become the faithful husband, the trustworthy employee, the patient mother, the loving sibling, and the generous giver. Imagine a society of adults raised with good moral character, who submit to a loving God in humility. This foundation is steadfast and secure.

What you sow, you will reap. It's ancient wisdom from God's holy Word that is so pertinent to our lives today. If you sow an apple seed, you won't get an avocado plant; you'll reap an apple tree. Once we made the decision to homeschool, my father-in-law, Dr. John McTernan, affirmed my decision with a wise analogy that still sticks with me today. He said that raising children is like taking care of seedlings. In order to take care of those little plants, you need to put them in a greenhouse and give them water, sun, and shelter, so they have the chance to grow into strong, healthy plants. However, if you put that seedling into a harsh environment, the likelihood of that seedling becoming a secure, robust plant, able to withstand the elements, is unlikely. Your children are like seedlings that need love, nurture, and protection. They need to be taught how to stand strong when exposed to ruthless environments.

As an American citizen, I am truly thankful to have religious freedom, and the liberty to teach my children about our faith at home. The right to decide how our children are educated is one of the most basic human rights, yet there are countries that do not agree with this. My family believes the Bible is the source of all wisdom and the basis of where good character comes from, and yet it is banned from public schools. Schools in our generation seem to accept everything but the Bible. They will tolerate gender-identity education by LGBT groups, allow books about witchcraft, provide books about violent gangs, and promote evolution—but will not accept the Bible. In fact, many schools today are not just unaccepting of Christians, they are hostile. I've read countless articles of Christian students being punished or expelled for bringing a Bible to school, praying before a meal, or wearing a shirt with a Bible verse on it.

As a homeschooling parent, you have the necessary environment to disciple your child in the ways of the Lord. The culture of your home is dictated by you, not opposing forces. You have the freedom and privilege of sharing your faith on a daily basis with your children. You also have the time needed to read the Bible together, pray together, worship together with music, share how God is working in your life, answer questions, and lovingly guide the child throughout the day. Deuteronomy 11:18-19 says, "Fix these words of mine in your hearts and minds; tie them as symbols on your hands and bind them on your foreheads. Teach them to your children, talking about them when you sit at home and when you walk along the road, when you lie down and when you get up."

Our job as parents, whether we homeschool or not, is to train our children while they are young, so when they are old they will be God-honoring, well-functioning, purpose-driven adults who care about those around them, who are able to be the salt and light in this world. This is a tremendous responsibility, but the good news is that we are not alone. When you rely on the Lord, He promises to be close to you and help you.

Practical Lessons for Life

I hesitate to write the word "practical" because I believe that the training and good character that have been mentioned are extremely practical. However, for the sense of relating the word to its common usage, I will make my next point. One practical benefit I came across when homeschooling was the ability to teach my child healthy eating habits. When my child was in kindergarten and first grade, as I stated earlier, he was allowed to make food choices on his own in the cafeteria. The problem with that was that the school was supplying unhealthy items and not monitoring the children's intake of sugar, dyes, and artificial ingredients, all substances that can have a negative effect on the body and brain.

With homeschooling, I utilized a daily trip to the grocery store to show my child how to find and read the ingredient label, and how to choose what is best for the body. One activity I did (inspired by the physician Dr. Sears) to demonstrate how to choose healthy bread was to hold two different types of white bread, one in each hand. I asked my son, "You want to be strong and healthy, don't you?" "Yes, of course," was the reply. I had him hold a loaf of bleached white flour Wonder Bread and an unbleached white flour loaf with all natural ingredients in it. He could feel the difference in weight. Then I asked him, "Now, do you want your muscles to feel like the Wonder Bread or the healthy bread?" The wonder bread was extremely "wimpy" compared to the healthier white bread. The choice was obvious. Point made!

A simple trip to the grocery store also provided lessons in how I budget for and plan the meals. This hands-on health study sprouted my son's interest in cooking, and I was able to teach him how to prepare meals. Because he typically finished his lessons in the early afternoon, he enjoyed having the time to prepare the evening meal on occasion!

Another very important practical skill taught in our home is responsibility. This can be taught to a child as young as age three. Our children have chores that they are responsible for, appropriate to their age, and the expectation is that they follow through with this responsibility or there will be an unpleasant consequence. One school semester, my oldest son was responsible for bringing all the recyclables to the garage after dinner each night except Sunday. If he did this consistently each week, he was rewarded (for example, by having a friend over). If not, he had something withheld, like not having screen time. This teaches the value of being dependable, working hard, and helps the home to function well, too!

Your child can learn many practical lessons at home, including how to use a fire extinguisher, do laundry (and be responsible for doing their own!), care for a garden, serve a neighbor, change a tire, balance a budget, or start a home-based business.

Family Bonding

As a new mom, I desired to have the family closeness that I witnessed in other homeschool families I met. I saw children gladly obeying their mothers, older siblings cheerfully helping their younger siblings, and children laughing along with their parents at inside jokes. This is a direct contrast to the typical American family you'd see on today's TV shows, where it's common for the children to disrespect and rebel against their parents, often making them look stupid, and where the siblings constantly argue or put each other down.

Since making the decision to homeschool, we do not have a perfect, happy-go-lucky family, but I can tell you that the bonds that have formed in my family are strong in comparison to what it would be if we chose not to homeschool. I can say that with confidence, because just 6 months ago I enrolled our oldest into public school and witnessed a dramatic change in his demeanor towards his family after doing so. He started treating his brothers rudely, talking disrespectfully to me, was embarrassed to be seen with us, and progressively grew distant and disengaged. I pulled him out to homeschool again, and within a month we saw exponential changes in his character for the better. He enjoys spending time with his family, engages with my husband and I in discussions, helps around the house willingly, and will actually *gasp* let me hug him again. I am incredibly thankful to God for those positive changes.

Homeschoolers spent a lot of quality time together, experiencing life together. It's through this time spent that parents are able to better understand their child, and the relationship grows. Families in close proximity, working and sharing life together, inevitably will have discord as well, but it is in those moments that parents have opportunity to turn those moments into a lesson of reconciliation and humility. I correct those behaviors, and my sons learn to resolve things in a godly manner.

From my personal experience, homeschooling has allowed my sons more time with each other and to bond with their baby brother. I emphasize to my sons that their brothers are their best friends for life, and to treat each other well. They enjoy playing together, reading together, drawing together, conducting science experiments together, and wrestling together.

I'm thankful that my children have a relationship with me that allows them to trust me and come to me whenever they want. I love that they can ask me for advice or questions about the world and that I can answer them, rather than their peers or another adult that may have a completely different value set than I do. My children and I have similar senses of humor and make each other laugh, and we have the approachability to discuss issues without being mocked or jeered at. My kids and I have open dialogue, and part of this is being authentic with them. I need to be humble before my children when I mess things up and ask for their forgiveness. It's all part of doing life together, and I love having a family to do life with. You get to know your children intimately. It's precious, valuable time together, and you can't replace that with anything else.

Produces a Love of Learning—Lifelong Learning!

Back when I was in school I remember loving my social time, but in general, school itself was boring, and a burden on my enjoyment as a child. I didn't see school from the perspective of learning; I just saw it as something I needed to do. I also didn't feel like my individual needs were met and was often afraid to ask questions. I remember not having enough time to spend time on the projects that interested me the most. For example, I would just get started on a still-life painting and need to drop everything to go to my next class. It took me several art classes just to finish just one painting.

I attended seven different schools growing up, and my favorite was that English boarding school I mentioned (go figure!). There, I was allowed to pursue my subjects of interest thoroughly, taking just three classes. I thought I was getting off easy at first! These A-Level classes, though, were rigorous, prestigious, and intended to be the launch into university. The teachers didn't condescend to the students; they taught as if talking to adults. I was asked intelligent questions and forced to think and prepare answers. The exams given were all essay format. This taught me to be prepared, as multiple choice did not exist as backup. I was given the time necessary to really delve deep into the subjects I loved the most: English, art and design, and history of art. For the first time in my schooling years, a love for learning was awakened in me.

This is what I hope to accomplish for my children as we homeschool. I want to allow them the time to pursue their passions, ask questions, problem-solve, and search for answers. At home, my children are away from social distractions and the negative opinions of others (such as being called a nerd for loving to read). They are truly able to think and process for themselves. This combination of having the time and encouragement to focus on their interests will allow their desire for obtaining knowledge and skills to grow.

When my eldest son gets into a hobby, he gets ALL in to it. He is one of those people that will concentrate heavily on a passion for a good amount of time, and then after about a year of that, he will have a new interest and focus heavily on that. You may see this in your children, too. As a toddler, he loved Thomas the Tank Engine, and wanted everything to do with Thomas. He played with the trains and memorized all fifty or so of their names. As he got a bit older, he was into Beyblades, which are competitive spinning tops. He collected as many as he could, found out everything he could about the features and physics of each type of Beyblade, and interchanged parts to create entirely new ones. He then started teaching all his friends about them and recommended which ones they should get.

Homeschooling has been great for him because he is able to have the freedom to delve deeply into the projects and subjects he loves, like reading, chemistry, drawing, fixing things, and, most recently, scooter tricks. A question I love to ask my kids is, "What would you like to learn about?" Asking this question helps me to understand how I can best plan lessons of interest, and allows us to dig for answers together, creating a unit study out of it. We have discovered the most fascinating things from this simple question.

Homeschoolers have a beautiful gift: the opportunity to explore their passions, unhindered, which ignites ideas, sparks creativity, and produces a love for learning!

Additionally, the enthusiasm you show will be contagious; it is the key to a successful homeschool. If you are an eager learner and can be positive in your approach, you will create excitement for learning in your child that will go far beyond the schooling years into adulthood. Combine this with teaching from exciting texts that have your child's particular interests in mind, and they will be hooked on gaining knowledge that will last a lifetime!

Problem-Solving Skills

Homeschooling allows a child the time necessary to adequately think through and solve problems. Thomas Edison and Benjamin Franklin were both homeschooled and given the time needed to work on projects and problems until they found the answers themselves—and look at the results of their hard work! We might not have electricity or light bulbs in our homes without what they discovered through problem-solving skills.

Results Look Good

The homeschooled child may have an environment in which he thrives, but how will he do as a teen entering college, or as an adult pursuing a career? Will there be any struggles or disadvantages to them having been homeschooled?

The most recent comprehensive study of the academic performance of homeschoolers was conducted in 2009, by the Home School Legal Defense Association (HSLDA) and National Home Education Research Institute (NHERI). They surveyed 11,739 homeschooling students and their families from all 50 states through 15 well-known independent testing services. The results show that homeschoolers, on average, score 37 percentile points above public school students on standardized achievement tests.[xiv]

NHERI did a study in 2014 comparing the results of the SAT exam and found that the homeschooled students. on average, scored well above the publicly-educated students. Dr Brian D. Ray reports: "Some 13,549 homeschool seniors had the following mean scores: 567 in critical reading, 521 in mathematics, and 535 in writing (College Board, 2014a). The mean SAT scores for all college-bound seniors in 2014 were 497 in critical reading, 513 in mathematics, and 487 in writing (College Board, 2014b). The homeschool students' SAT scores were 0.61 standard deviation higher in reading, 0.26 standard deviation higher in mathematics, and 0.42 standard deviation higher in writing than those of all college-bound seniors taking the SAT, and these are notably large differences."[xv]

In 2012, Mary Beth Bolle-Brummond and Roger D. Wessel published their research findings in the *Journal of Research in Education*. They examined adults in college who were home educated. They conducted a five-year, in-depth study of five homeschooled students from a variety of backgrounds. They evaluated their transitional first year of college, and then again five years later to examine the influence of their homeschool backgrounds on their college experiences. What they found was that the students were well prepared both socially and academically. One participant commented that many of his core classes seemed to be a repeat of high school coursework. The researchers found that the students were self-motivated, organized learners and often the leaders in the class. All of them worked for pay at some point during their college education, and all of them were involved in extracurricular clubs or sports. One student indicated that homeschooling allowed him to be less influenced by stereotypes, allowing him to develop friends from various backgrounds. Although they had to adjust to a formal educational setting, the researchers concluded, "We found that they experienced college in many of the same ways that other, non-homeschooled students, did. In most regards, their undergraduate experiences were unidentifiable from the overall student population: they were normal college students" (p. 247).[xvi]

From my own interactions with adults who have been homeschooled, I've found that they are not only pleased with their experience but would want to homeschool their own children. Each of the people I spoke to displayed self-confidence, a purpose-driven life, and excellence in a variety of areas. Of course, my most immediate source is my husband who wrote the foreword for this book. He was homeschooled during middle school, a very awkward phase developmentally for most pre-teens. My husband's favorite school years where the ones in which he was homeschooled, and he attributes his love of learning to his mother. He also says she piqued his interest in science and astronomy. He ended up graduating from public high school with honors, studied physics in his undergraduate work, and received a full scholarship to graduate school to study aerospace engineering. He is now a NASA Postdoctoral Fellow at Marshall Space Flight Center. Above all of these achievements, though, I see his integrity. He is a man of character. His parents instilled into him biblical values from integrating Bible into his home education. In the Testimonials section of this book, I have included other anecdotes of those who share how homeschooling shaped them for life.

To be fair, there are those who did not enjoy their homeschool experience, and of those people, the common factor seems to be that they were not engaged by their parent and given opportunities outside the home. This neglect is not common, and should not be. If you choose to homeschool, it must be for the benefit of your child, not driven by fear, selfishness, or any other ungodly desire. I believe the most successful homeschooled children are those who were raised in a loving home with their interest in mind, given various opportunities, and with parents who relied on the Lord as their strength.

I was exceedingly encouraged by the stories of the people I spoke with, but I wanted to give you a more informed perspective than a selection of people I interviewed, so I did some research to find out what the results look like for adults who were homeschooled. The most current large-scale research survey of adults who were home educated was conducted in 2003 by NHERI. The study surveyed over 7,300 adults who had been homeschooled and concluded that most were college-educated, engaged in a wide variety of occupations, and are actively involved in community service.[xvii]

Professional football player Tim Tebow and his siblings were homeschooled until college, and all five of the Tebow children went on to receive college scholarships. Tim was the first underclassman ever to be awarded the Heisman Trophy for most outstanding player in collegiate football. He earned the Maxwell Award as the nation's top football player twice. He also won the Davey O'Brien Award as the nation's best quarterback and the James E. Sullivan Award as the nation's most outstanding amateur athlete in any sport. In a one-hour documentary about Tebow that aired on ESPN, Tim is seen studying the Bible as part of his high school homeschool curriculum. As an adult, Tebow prays with his football team before and after practice. ESPN producer Ken Murrah said of Tebow, "I knew he was a good football player in his strength, size, and unique skills, but I was amazed at his natural ability and maturity to speak publicly, go into schools, be comfortable in being a role model, and talk so openly about his faith." Tim shares his experience as a homeschooler with young homeschooled kids in his book titled *Know Who You Are. Live Like It Matters.* He has advocated for homeschooled students through the "Tim Tebow Bill," a legislative act which would allow homeschooled students to participate in public school athletics. The bill has been approved in many states across America and will benefit the 2 million homeschoolers across America.

Entrepreneur Emerson Spartz, a Notre Dame graduate, started his online business in 1999 as a 12-year-old homeschooler. He created a website, MuggleNet.com, and gathered a team of 120 people who contributed from around the world (and who, incidentally, had no idea of how old he was at the time!). MuggleNet quickly became the #1 Harry Potter fan site, and by 2005 it was generating a six-figure income. Spartz says about homeschooling, "I figured I could always go back to school if I didn't like it, but it turned out to be the best decision I ever made. I started [the website] a few months after I began homeschooling. I never expected it to get so big." Emerson co-authored the NY Times best-selling children's book *MuggleNet.com's What Will Happen in Harry Potter 7*. He is also the CEO of Dose, a digital media company that produces the *Morning Dose* TV show and churns out social media posts aimed at being funny, inspirational, and mind-blowing.[xviii]

Homeschooling Has Stood the Test of Time

I found it encouraging to learn that the model of an individualized home education is nothing new, despite reports that people educating from home in the 80s were called "pioneers." It simply wasn't popular after the 50s and gained a resurgence of popularity in the 90s. Home education goes way back in time and has produced many famous, well-educated individuals, confident of who they were, and whose natural aptitudes were strengthened at home. Some of these acclaimed persons include: Alexander the Great, George Washington, Abraham Lincoln, Winston Churchill, Blaise Pascal, Thomas Edison, Wilbur Wright and Albert Einstein![xix]

One of the most famous scientists of all time, Albert Einstein, was unhappy in school. His disdain for school came from the compulsion to do the work required and a tendency to do things his own way. He wrote that the spirit of discovery and creative thought were lost in strict rote learning.[xx] In the book *Albert Einstein: A Biography*,[xxi] Einstein is described as being an exceptionally bright, self-motivated learner who could get good scores when he wanted to, but who refused to waste his time with school activities in which he saw little value." While not completely homeschooled in a strict sense, Einstein began self-study by age 10, considering this to be "his real studies . . . done at home."[xxii] Outside school hours, he taught himself algebra from books his parents purchased, worked math puzzles, and learned complicated mathematical concepts like Euclidian geometry (the study of points, lines, and surfaces). By the age of 15, Albert had mastered differential and integral calculus, a higher form of mathematics used to solve problems in physics and engineering. While most of us won't encounter genius at this level, it's interesting to note that Einstein's frustration in school wasn't due to a lack of intellect, but rather that his intellect was being suppressed. Home education gave him the freedom to pursue his interests and excel in life.

Homeschoolers Save Taxpayers Money

Homeschoolers benefit the community! Taxpayers are required to pay an average of $11,732 per student, according to NHERI, plus capital expenditures.[xxiii] The average homeschool family usually spends about $600 annually for their child's education. According to NHERI, "Families engaged in home-based education are not dependent on public, tax-funded resources for their children's education. The finances associated with their homeschooling likely represent over $27 billion that American taxpayers do not have to spend, annually, since these children are not in public schools." While this is not a direct benefit to homeschoolers, I found it interesting.

❦

As you can see, there really is a plethora of benefits for the homeschooling parent, their children, and even the community! Considering the benefits listed, are you encouraged? Which of these benefits excite you most? Did anything surprise you?

In the following chapter, I will guide you through the decision-making process, you'll read how God answered my prayer from chapter 1, and I'll help you set goals for each of your children so you can proactively take charge of their whole-person development.

Chapter 4

Purposeful Planning

You may love what you have read so far about homeschooling but doubt whether it's something *you* can do. Or perhaps you are undecided as to whether it is what is best for your family. This chapter is designed to guide you through the decision-making process and help you create a purposeful plan suited for your family. This part is best read while the kids are in bed and your cell phone is on silent, so you can process without distractions.

Making the Decision

The Bible tells us that the first step in making a decision is to seek Him first, and everything else will fall into place. Spend some time right now, in the stillness, with the Lord. Meditate on His words, "Cast all your anxiety on Him, because He cares for you" (1 Peter 5:7), and ask Him to reveal to you what you should do for each of your children.

Proverbs 8:17 says, "I love those who love me; and those who seek me find me." I'm urging you today to seek the Lord with this decision for your family and ask Him what it is He is calling you to do. He will direct your steps. Proverbs 3:6 encourages us with these words, "Trust in the Lord with all your heart and lean not on your own understanding. In all your ways submit to him, and he will make your paths straight."

Once you have sought the Lord, listen for an answer. If you're a mom of young children, you may be thinking, "How will I ever hear from God if I can't seem to get any quiet time alone?" Don't worry. The Lord knows exactly how you feel and will meet you right where you are, as he has done for me.

As I mentioned earlier in the book, I was troubled about whether or not to pull our oldest son out of public school. In just a couple short months, I had some serious issues concerning the education and environment of this school. I prayed about it, and God gave me an answer just when I least expected to hear from Him: in the middle of watching my baby son crawl. The Lord clearly told me that just as I had to physically rescue my toddler from putting harmful objects in his mouth as he crawled, so I needed to physically remove my son from the public school environment. My toddler may cry when I pick him up, but I know it's to save him from potential danger. My oldest son also was not happy when I chose to withdraw him from school, but because I heard the Lord clearly I felt confident that I was doing what was best for him. As I said, it didn't take long for him to readjust at home and to thrive in that environment. I was stunned that the

78

Lord answered my prayer right in the middle of my "mommy duty," in a way that I could understand—and I trust God will answer you in a way that is relevant to you as well.

Take a moment to jot down any thoughts you are currently processing, and what you believe the Lord is saying to you.

℘

You may be doubting your ability to teach your children. Please know that God wants your heart—not perfection. He will use you if you let Him, and He is capable of so much more than we can imagine! I distinctly remember the fears in the beginning that kept me from saying "yes" to the idea of homeschooling: one was fear of failure, and the other was the thought that once I made this decision I was locked into it for the rest of my child's educational years. May I encourage you to not allow fear or doubt to hold you back? I never could have imagined, years ago, how much I'd grow in the process of homeschooling. I have made many mistakes, but God is faithful, and He has given me everything I need to teach to the best of my ability, to keep going, and to actually enjoy it!

Trust the Father with this decision. He cares about you, and He cares more about the welfare of your children than you do! (I have to remind myself of that often.) A favorite Bible verse of mine is found in Isaiah 40:11: "He gathers the lambs in his arms and carries them close to his heart; he gently leads those that have young."

A method that helped me when making the decision of whether to homeschool or not was to make a comparison chart. My husband and I did this exercise separately, then we came together to compare notes and have a discussion. If you are single, you may do this exercise on your own or with someone who knows you and your child well. If you are married, it is vitally important that you and your spouse are in agreement about your child's educational path. I encourage you to have your spouse write out their own chart, then when you have both finished you can compare and discuss. The process of brainstorming and creating a visual display of your thoughts will help you to see the comparisons quite clearly. You may be surprised to see how heavily one outweighs the other. I have gone through this process with many difficult decisions, and I've found it to be quite helpful to me as a visual processor.

Here's how my husband and I did it: we folded a piece of paper in half, creating two columns. At the top of the left column we wrote "positives," and on the right we wrote "negatives." Then, under each category, we listed as many pros and cons of homeschooling as we could think of. (I'll include a sample in the Resources section.) It might also be helpful to prepare a separate sheet listing the positives and negatives of alternate forms of schooling.

Once you have made your comparison chart and can see both sides, it's time to analyze whether any of the negatives can be changed to positives. For example, a negative could be that your weakness is mathematics, and you are hesitant to teach it. You could turn that negative into a positive by finding a tutor or an instructional DVD to teach math instead. If the negative is something that cannot be changed, consider how it will affect you and your family. Is it worth pursuing, despite that aspect?

One common "negative" may be that you will lose time to yourself. This is a fact that cannot be changed, but I would argue that it is, indeed, worth the sacrifice of your time and effort. You can certainly invest in yourself (see chapter 6, "Be good to yourself!") as you invest your energy into diligently training your children. This pursuit is worth the effort to yield an abundant harvest. Scripture has a lot to say about reaping what you sow, and I believe this teaching is completely relevant to how we raise our children. One such verse is in Galatians 6:9: "And let us not grow weary of doing good, for in due season we will reap, if we do not give up." (ESV) The time you commit to homeschooling, when done well, will allow you to spend unrushed quality time with your children, strengthening your bonds with them and creating memories your whole family will look back on with joy.

As you look at your own comparison chart of homeschooling pros and cons, if your negatives column happens to weigh more heavily, please don't let that discourage you. I ask that you continue to read this book, as you may find solutions to the very things you listed as possible drawbacks.

Casting a Vision

Now that you have spent time with the Lord and listed items onto your comparison chart, it is time to envision what your ideal homeschool and family life looks like. If you are married, again, I encourage you to invite your spouse to take part in this. Allow your mind the freedom to think without any negative excuses to distract you from this process. To quote Henry Ford, "If you think you can do a thing or think you can't do a thing, you're right." With a positive outlook, imagine the dreams you have for your family. Are you mission-minded and desire to have your children learn to serve by helping others together? Do you have a child that wants to become a professional athlete and would benefit from having the flexibility to spend daytime hours training for their sport? Perhaps you imagine a home life where your children begin the day with time in the Bible, learning how to treat their siblings with love, or you're a scientist who believes you can teach your elementary-aged students the basics of physics. Or maybe you are a painter who wants the freedom to travel to Monet's garden in France while teaching art history, French, cooking, and painting! (Ok, it's a stretch—but that's my dream, don't squelch it!)

After you have spent some time dreaming, use a goal sheet (perhaps like the sample in the Resources section of the book) to help you determine how you can make these dreams a reality while considering the needs of each of your children. Make a copy for each child. Envision how you would like them to grow. The goals you list for each of your children can be both immediate and long-term goals. Make sure your goals are SMART: Specific, Measurable, Achievable, Realistic, and Timely. (You can search "SMART goals" online for more help.) Pray for each child and consider each of these areas: academic, physical, social, and spiritual.

For example, for your child you may write the following:

- Academic: dislikes reading
  - Goal: to produce a love for reading
  - Ideas: Take them to the library each Monday to do our lessons and check out books for the week. Allow them to select 5-10 books on their own. Create a book basket where library books can "live" during the week, ready for their free reading time. Set up a reading reward chart.
- Physical: strong swimmer
  - Goal: compete in the Olympics
  - Ideas: Swim 3x/week; homeschool to have enough time to practice, travel for competitions and tryouts, and join in team training times if accepted.
- Social: needs help choosing friends wisely
  - Goal: to know how to discern good character and be a good friend
  - Ideas: Memorize Proverbs 13:20 and help find friends that will have a positive impact. Go to different social events, including homeschool field trips and get to know the other families. Serve together as a family at church. Invite children whom I think would be a good friend for them. Consult *Young Peacemaker* by Corlette Sande as a tool.
- Spiritual: lacking daily devotion time
  - Goal: to have a time set aside each day for personal devotions, doing this consistently without being reminded
  - Ideas: Buy the devotional book *3-Minute Devotions for Girls* by Janice Thompson or *3-Minute Devotions for Guys* by Glenn Hascall and have them read it while I'm preparing breakfast each day.

Next, write a list of those areas where you'll need help achieving the goals you have for your child. Are you weak in writing? Does science scare you? Do you have a child that has special needs? Don't allow your areas of weakness to discourage you; there are plenty of resources available to help. For example, if you need support teaching math, you can purchase an instructional DVD math curriculum (such as Math U See or Teaching Textbooks), hire a tutor, or have your child take an online class (Time4Learning, Math U See, CTCMath). You can also join a local homeschool co-op that is teaching the class, or ask someone you know such as a veteran homeschooler, retired teacher, or a willing grandparent to teach that subject. Pray and have faith that God will provide the necessary help. I've already mentioned that my area of weakness happens to be math, and when I heard God's calling to pull my son from public school the second time I dreaded the thought of teaching the subject. My husband is excellent at math but, with his new position at work, he didn't have time to teach him. I prayed about it, and during my search for homeschool groups I was introduced to a retired NASA scientist who was available to tutor math. I couldn't have asked for a better answer to prayer!

Does this give you a clearer idea of what you are hoping for your children and family? Do you believe that homeschooling will help you to achieve those goals?

Now that you've thought about the goals for your children and imagined what your ideal homeschool would look like, it's time to think about what you enjoy doing. Yes, you read that right: YOU. Has it been a while since you've thought about that?! What inspires you? Are you creative? Do you play an instrument? Do you love observing nature? Are you a history buff? What are your gift and talents, and how can you share these with your children? What would you enjoy learning about? Take note of these. They'll help give you the motivation you need to homeschool with passion! If you're excited about teaching, the overflow of your enthusiasm will inspire your children to be willing, happy pupils who are eager to learn.

Taking the time to get your child's input is invaluable. Find out what their favorite school subject is, and why. Ask what they would like to learn about. This will help you to guide their learning in a way that is inspiring to them. Knowing what their interests are will also help you to figure out what their particular bent is. God created all our children uniquely, with a plan and purpose, and as you spend time with your child you'll begin to see the gifts, abilities, and plans He has for your child. The beautiful thing about you being their teacher is, as you discover their areas of strength, you will be able to nurture and develop those gifts in a way that only the deep love of a parent can. Every child longs to have the praise of their parents. You are able to inspire your child on a deep emotional level; even if you don't think you're getting through to them—you are!

If your child says they don't have a favorite school subject (or if they're too young to know what that means), use what you already know about your child to encourage learning. For example, your child may have a fascination with superheroes. You can use that zeal for superheroes to teach multiple lessons. For Bible, use the superhero theme to teach biblical concepts like good versus evil and how to combat evil using scripture (the sword of the Spirit). You can tell them Jesus is mightier than all the superheroes' strength combined! Hide printed scripture verses around the room relating to Jesus's power; for example, Jesus has power to perform miracles (Matthew 8:27), Jesus has the power of eternal life (John 17:2). Then have your child go on a treasure hunt while dressed as a superhero. When they find a verse, read it out loud to them and have them say it back. For writing, assign a creative writing piece based on what superpower they would like. For art, they can learn how to draw a comic strip.

If you are thinking, "I'm just not a creative person!" then I recommend searching websites like Pinterest. They have a host of creative ideas for homeschoolers. You'll receive more ideas in the following chapters as well.

☙

If you've made it this far into the book, chances are you've made the decision to homeschool and you're ready to begin the adventure! I'm excited for you! This is a journey like no other, where you are proactively taking charge of your child's education and whole-person training. You are investing in a relationship with your child that will leave a lasting legacy and bear good fruit, if you determine to do it well, relying on the Lord as your strength and guide.

Just as a builder needs all the right tools to do the job, so does the homeschool teacher. You should now have a framework for what your homeschool will look like, the reason for why you will do it, and clear goals mapped out for each child. You have a good foundation set to launch your homeschool on the right track. The next chapter will give you practical, easy-to-follow steps to get started.

Spend some time in prayer before reading on, thanking Him for giving you the gift of your children and asking for guidance and His blessing on each of your children.

Part II

How to Homeschool with Confidence

Chapter 5

Getting Started

Yay! So you've decided to jump all in! Just like preparing for a marathon, you will need to prepare for the race you're about to run. You have your goals in sight, and now you need to start working out. But where do you start?

Legal Steps

Begin by going to the Homeschool Legal Defense Association's website (hslda.org) to look up the homeschool laws for your state. Each state has its own requirements for homeschoolers, and you need to be sure that you comply with those laws. For example, when I lived in Pennsylvania, I had to submit a notarized letter of intent and a list of objectives to the school district each year, and I was required to compile a portfolio for each child throughout the year. Some states require that the student be tested every other year, while others require you to register under a "cover school." These cover schools will take care of state legal requirements, and they often provide additional instruction and activities for homeschooled children. HSLDA recommends that you keep records of your child's work no matter what your state requirements are. More detailed advice on what records to maintain are listed on their website.

If your child is currently enrolled in private or public school, the HSLDA site recommends, "If you are going to start homeschooling after the school year is over, and your child is considered enrolled for the following year, we recommend that you withdraw your child before the next school year begins, so that the school does not mark your child as absent or truant."

I recommend becoming a member of HSLDA. You will receive a teacher card in the mail that identifies you as a homeschool teacher, which gives you access to many discounts. You'll also have access to online classes and receive individualized advice and legal support from a team of qualified attorneys 24/7! The direct link for membership is membership.hslda.org.

Don't allow the regulations to intimidate you. Even though I began homeschooling in Pennsylvania, a state that has heavy restrictions on homeschoolers, I found that once I understood what to do it wasn't burdensome. I actually enjoyed having a documented portfolio of my son's work each year as a reminder of all we had done, and it became a wonderful keepsake for years to come.

I now homeschool in Alabama, where a portfolio is not required, but I have chosen to compile one for each child anyway since I greatly enjoy having this keepsake to look back on. I plan to give them to my children once they've grown.

Find Community

Find other homeschoolers in your community and learn as much as you can from them. Don't be afraid to ask questions, such as what their favorite books are for teaching, if they have any books they'd be willing to share with you, what ideas they may have for field trips, and what local homeschool groups you can join. Find someone willing to show you their homeschool room, lesson plans, and any other items required in your state. Ask to see their curriculum. Find out what worked well for them, and what didn't.

In our early homeschool years, I was part of a Christian homeschool support group that was particularly helpful to me, and from whom I learned a great deal. Our meetings were held at a church and consisted of prayer time for our families, sharing ideas and resources, and an occasional speaker (typically veteran homeschoolers). I definitely recommend finding a support group in your area—or starting one up!

Placement Tests

Before deciding on which curriculum to purchase, it is helpful to have your child tested, particularly for math and language arts. Some placement tests are provided for free through curriculum providers, such as Saxon for math or Sonlight for language arts. Alternatively (or in addition), you could have your child take a standardized test for a fee, which typically includes both math and language arts assessments. You can find a list of homeschool publishers and accredited standardized testing services in the Resources section. Knowing how your child scores will be extremely helpful in determining which books you select for them.

Choosing Curriculum

There are so many options, and that is a happy problem! I remember attending my first homeschool conference in Harrisburg, Pennsylvania, and being amazed at the massive building. The curriculum area alone was rows and rows of tables showcasing books and other homeschool materials. The options seemed endless! I had no idea how popular homeschooling was, and I felt both excited and overwhelmed that there were a great many curriculum options to choose from.

When deciding on which curriculum to use, it's important to know which subjects you'll be teaching, and at what grade level, before you shop. With homeschooling, one size doesn't have to fit all—you have the option to allow your child to move ahead if he's ready, or spend extra weeks or months learning a subject if necessary. You could have a 2nd grader (by public school age) whose learning levels are 3rd grade for English and 1st grade for math, for example. There's no right or wrong when it comes to tailoring to what is needed for your child!

Also, it is helpful (but not necessary right away) to decide what type of method you'll want to teach from (see Methods section for further explanation). Do you want all the lesson plans laid out for you, or do you prefer to plan your own schedule? Do you want to teach all your children from a curriculum that works for multiple age levels, or not? You should also decide if there's a subject you would like to outsource, whether to a grandparent, tutor, homeschool co-op class, computer program, instructional DVD, online classroom, etc.

Consider what's important for your family to be learning this year. Do you want the curriculum to have a missions focus? Do you want to include a curriculum that teaches from a Christian perspective? Do you want to include a specific subject that's not necessarily in a boxed curriculum set, such as robotics, character development, art history, or purity education?

If you enjoy books like I do, it's all too easy to go book-buying crazy, so having thought these things through ahead of time will definitely help you to choose a curriculum that suits your family's needs, while helping you stay on budget.

Attend a Homeschool Conference

One of my favorite ways to find curriculum and materials for homeschooling is to attend a homeschool convention. This way you are able to meet the representatives of each curriculum provider and ask them questions on the spot. You will also be able to open up the books and see the contents. There are many different conferences to choose from, such as Teach Them Diligently, a conference hosted in multiple cities across the U.S. every year. Look closer to home if these locations are not convenient for you--almost every state has a conference you can attend. (A simple internet search for "homeschool convention in [state]" will be enlightening.) I've included a list of the most well-known conferences in the resources section as a reference.

All of the homeschool conferences I've been to have benefitted me as a wife, parent, and teacher. I've learned a great deal and have been refreshed each time. A generalized layout is a three-day event that includes well-known speakers, booths representing various curricula, and representatives of other opportunities for homeschoolers like camps, colleges, missions organizations, music classes, etc. Typically, the conferences also include a children's program, which my children have always enjoyed. They found the programs engaging and fun, and they were eager to return the next day.

You can choose to attend one in your state, or take the family on a fun trip to another state, depending on which conference or location interests you the most. I love connecting with other homeschool families from all over the USA.

One year we decided to attend an out-of-state convention instead of the in-state one we typically went to because it was held at a hotel with a water park! We ended up going with another family from our homeschool group and had an absolute blast. The kids had a supervised program while my husband, our friends, and I attended the conference with our friends during the day. We cut costs by taking turns preparing meals in our room equipped with a kitchen. The travel effort was worth it for the memories we made and knowledge we gained.

A practical recommendation I would make is to bring a roller cart with you. That way, if you purchase books along the way, you have an easy way to carry them throughout the day. It's also a good idea to look at the schedule of speakers before the conference begins and plan which sessions you'd like to attend; deciding this ahead of time will really help you save time. My husband and I circle the sessions we'd like to attend on separate sheets of paper, then we compare them. If we want to see different sessions scheduled at the same time, we break up and share notes afterward.

New Books

One year I ordered books from a convention, and they were shipped to my house for free. Receiving those books in the mail was so exciting for both my kids and myself that it became a tradition in our home to have the first day of school be a bit like Christmas. I wrap their new (or new-to-us) books and school supplies in wrapping paper and leave everything on the kitchen table for them to open in the morning. I love seeing their bright eyes and eager enthusiasm over receiving new study materials (—a mother's dream come true, ha!).

If you would like to buy your books new, you can do so at a convention, directly from a curriculum provider, or from an online retailer. Some retailers supply a range of curriculum sets; these companies include Rainbow Resource Inc., Christian Book Distributors (CBD), Timberdoodle, and Rock Solid Inc., to name a few. Each of these retailers also offers educational kits, games, and supplies. To purchase books directly from the curriculum provider, you can visit their website, or visit their booth at a convention. I have included a list of some of the top curriculum publishers at the back of the book, in the Resources section.

Finding Used Books

New homeschooling materials can be expensive, so as you make connections with other homeschool families, inquire if they would sell you their books when they are finished with them. You may also find a used homeschool book sale near you. If you do have one in your area, take advantage of this, because you will pay a fraction of the cost of new books. Just note that you most likely won't find new workbooks, so ask the person you are buying from if there is a workbook you need to go with the materials you are purchasing. For example, most math textbooks also have an accompanying workbook, and you'll want to know which one goes together.

One homeschool dad in our community set up a used homeschool book sale at a local church each year, where homeschool parents could sell their used books to others in the community. He would also allow students to set up booths to sell their handmade items. You may have something like this within your community; ask around. Again, you will be able to connect with other homeschoolers, ask them questions, and find great prices on books that have worked well for other families. If you cannot find one, look into options online. Amazon has used homeschool books, and Facebook has a number of "homeschool used books for sale" groups. Here are some examples:

- *Classical Conversations Used Materials Buy-Sell-Trade-Share*
- *Used Homeschool Books, Buy, Sell, Trade*
- *Sonlight Homeschool Curriculum USED books Sell-Swap-Share*
- *Abeka Used Curriculum for Sale*
- *My Father's World Curriculum Exchange*

Methods of Teaching

When I first started homeschooling, I knew which subjects I needed to teach, but I had no idea that there were different methods of instructing. I overheard other homeschoolers utter terminology like "Charlotte Mason" and "Classical" and felt lost—I had no idea what they were referring to. Let me save you some head-scratching! I'm going to give you a very simple introduction to different methods for teaching at home and some examples of each. This way you have a clear understanding and are prepared to answer others with confidence when they ask you what method you are using to teach.

Classical

The Classical method teaches how to learn and how to think. What I find most interesting about this method is that learning is taught according to the natural development of the child's brain. Learning is broken up into three stages: grammar, logic, and rhetoric. Classical Academic Press explains it well:

"In the grammar stage (K–6), students are naturally adept at memorizing through songs, chants, and rhymes. If you can get children in this stage to sing or chant something, they will remember it for a lifetime. In the dialectic or logic stage (grades 7–9), teenaged students are naturally more argumentative and begin to question authority and facts. They want to know the "why" of something—the logic behind it. During this stage, students learn reasoning, informal and formal logic, and how to argue with wisdom and eloquence. The rhetoric stage (grades 10–12) is naturally when students become independent thinkers and communicators. They study and practice rhetoric, which is the art of persuasive speaking and effective writing that pleases and delights the listener. Again, it is this approach to teaching students based on their developmental stage that makes this approach so very effective."[xxiv]

Aristotle, Sir Isaac Newton, C.S. Lewis, and Thomas Jefferson are just a few examples of great thinkers who were classically educated.

Classical Conversations (CC) is the world's largest classical Christian homeschool organization. Their motto is "To know God and make Him known." They have community groups for grades K-12 all over the world. The unique aspect of CC material is the synchronization. At every CC campus, no matter where you are in the world, every child is learning the same cyclical material over a three-year time span. That was great for us when we moved from Pennsylvania to Alabama. My kids were able to transition from where they left off into an environment they were already familiar with.

When we visited a Classical Conversations community for the first time, I was amazed by what the kids had memorized, all in a fun, engaging way. For example, by the end of the school year, the students in grades K-5 could sing a timeline of history, from creation all the way through to our current President!

Charlotte Mason

Charlotte Mason was a British educator who dedicated much of her life to improving education in the late 1800s. Her educational principles have become a popular homeschooling method. She describes education as "an atmosphere, a discipline, a life." Charlotte believed that the Bible was the primary source for all wisdom and knowledge. She also believed that teaching good habits at a young age, like focused attention, was of utmost importance. Her lessons would include time to ponder challenging problems, narration, story-based history taught chronologically, and observing nature. She taught children to memorize hymns, poems, and Scripture.

The website simplycharlottemason.com supplies curriculum and lesson plans using the Charlotte Mason method. These were developed by Sonya Shafer, a popular homeschool speaker and writer. She has researched and practiced the Charlotte Mason Method for over twenty years, beginning with training her four daughters.

Un-schooling

This approach has no set curriculum. The student is free to learn based on their interests. For example, if your child is interested in robots, they can research and discover all there is to learn about robots. Utilizing the books at a library, taking courses that pertain to that interest, and attending field trips will enhance this approach.

Brick and mortar/traditional

These are the terms for the method that is taught in many conventional classrooms today. It consists of having separate textbooks and workbooks for each subject. Students are required to read the material and answer questions about the content through multiple choice and fill-in-the blank questions. Quizzes and tests are often in the same format.

Unit studies

This is not necessarily a method, but I included it anyway since it is one of the common teaching tools. You'll hear the term used widely among homeschoolers. To teach a unit study, you will use all of the school subjects to focus on one particular topic. For example, to teach about Japan, students can read about the history of Japan (history), draw and label a map of Asia (geography), create a Haiku poem (language arts), create woodblock prints (art), learn the Japanese math trick of multiplying using lines (math), study the nature and climate of Japan (science), and eat Japanese food at a Hibachi restaurant (experience culture and for fun!).

Eclectic

An eclectic mix is not truly a method, either; it is a term meaning various methods are incorporated into your homeschool. You can teach unit studies while also using a classical teaching method; you can teach from a packaged curriculum and utilize resources from other curricula; or you can simply choose various books from different publishers.

Mapping Out Your School Year

First, purchase a planner that is laid out in a way that makes sense to you. Not all planners are created equal. I personally prefer planners that show the whole week on one page with plenty of space to write in. The planner I've most enjoyed using is designed just for the homeschool teacher; it's called *The Ultimate Homeschool Planner,* and it's published by Apologia. It gives you room to plan lessons for multiple children and contains valuable tips and encouragement for the homeschool parent. Apologia also makes planners for students, which is a great way to encourage independent learning, organization, and responsibility for completing assignments.

Once you have your planner, pencil in an idea of what your school year will look like. This plan can always be modified, but it helps to have a general academic calendar to work with. Frame things out according your state's requirements for educational days or hours, remembering that you can include field trips as credit. Schedule in when you'd like to start and finish the year, and when you would like to take breaks or vacation time. You may decide to school year-round, utilizing the myriad of educational opportunities available during the summer months and counting them as school days (like children's camps at universities and summer reading programs through Barnes & Noble or the library).

Once you have your framework, decide what your week might look like. For example, do you want your children to have Bible time every day after helping clean up breakfast? If so, pencil that in. Add any activities you have scheduled during the week. Once you have the items on your calendar, imagine what it would look like to live that out. Does your calendar look too full, or just about right?

Finally, you will need to lesson plan. Each homeschooling family does this differently. Some families prepare their lessons one week at a time, others one quarter at a time (or even longer!), while others follow built-in lesson plans that are part of their chosen curriculum. One is not better than the other, but no matter which method you use, don't leave planning to the last minute. This is a sure-fire way to leave you frazzled and discouraged. Once the kids are awake for the day and ready to go, it is very difficult to make a plan—so be sure you're ready in advance.

Setting Up Your Classroom and Gathering Materials

When I made the decision to homeschool, I lived in a small 900-square-foot apartment where there were two bedrooms and one central room that included the kitchen and living area. The kitchen table was our desk. I kept homeschool books on a shelf right next to the kitchen table and used a set of tall plastic drawers to organize my son's daily assignments, creating a workbox system (you can search online for more ideas on how to implement these in your homeschool). This worked well to keep materials organized and for him to be able to see what was assigned for the day.

A couple of years later, we moved into a three-bedroom house with a finished basement. It was exciting for me to have the extra space to create a separate homeschool room, and the kids loved it too. Here are three of my boys on their first day of school in the basement schoolroom:

My three-year-old felt special having a desk just like his big brothers. On the wall to the right I had a map of the world, and on the opposite end of the room we set up a cozy reading corner with a couch and bookshelf.

We schooled in there for the first few weeks but ended up doing most of our lessons at the kitchen table upstairs. A good portion of my time outside of teaching was spent in the kitchen, and we needed the kitchen sink and linoleum floors for conducting science experiments and messy art projects. It was also easier for me to be in the same room while they worked independently, so I could be there to answer questions rather than running downstairs.

Gradually, the map, the bookshelf, and all our books worked their way upstairs. I accepted that, at this stage of life, it was better for me to have a well-functioning room than to anxiously try to recreate a Martha Stewart model kitchen. With three little boys in a well-used space, it was practical to have the kitchen as our classroom. It wasn't aesthetically pleasing, but I learned to like it. I gave myself grace by not dismantling our entire homeschool room every time a guest came over. What I didn't expect was the interesting conversations that resulted from our guests seeing our sons' latest work on the wall! We hosted a Chinese student, a Buddhist, who asked what the Bible verse on the wall meant, a Russian couple that marveled over our son's homemade history timeline, and neighbors who enjoyed reading from our "thankful garland." Our kitchen wall displayed whatever it was we were working on that week, and it became a fun source of conversation for our guests rather than an embarrassment that my kitchen wasn't picture perfect.

I share all of that to tell you that the most important factor when deciding how to set up your school room is to have an environment that is conducive to learning, in a space that functions best for your family. You can have a separate school room in your home, or you may find your kitchen table works best, too. Either way, make sure to have a table space available to them that is free from clutter, and eliminate as many distractions as possible.

I recommend dedicating a space in your home to keep all the homeschool books and supplies and investing in containers and bookshelves to organize them. You will also need access to a computer, printer, binders, whiteboard or chalkboard, hole punch, and the basic school supplies like pencils, pens, papers, scissors, glue, etc. Although it's not essential, having a laminator will come in handy for many purposes, such as creating reusable worksheets.

Make sure to have a good home library so your children can have a wide variety of literature to read and reference. To build up your library, ask your parents or other homeschool veterans if they have any books to pass on to you; buy used books on Amazon; or shop at your local library book sale. Take time to visit the library and allow your children to check out books. The simple act of selecting their own books will inspire reading.

Provide areas around the house for your child to get creative! We have a basket next to our piano filled with small instruments that even our one-year-old enjoys playing with. It contains a harmonica, maracas, slide whistle, xylophone, tambourine, a jaw-harp, and some others. In our kitchen pantry, we have craft supplies in separate plastic containers—beads, fun shape-cutting scissors, construction paper, glue, sequins, stickers, and other artsy items. In our living room, we have a storage shelf that houses puzzles and board games.

Whatever your child is interested in, whether it be robotics, drawing, or engineering, supply the tools and time necessary to be able to focus, study, and learn in a hands-on manner. My oldest son is interested in fixing bikes. Since he has been given time and space in our garage to dismantle a bike and put it back together, he has quite a lot of knowledge about how bikes work and how to fix them. He's used his skills to help fix bikes in our neighborhood.

Lastly, if it pleases you, decorate your homeschool area in a way that suits your style and is engaging to your child. There are some fun ideas on Pinterest to get your creative juices flowing. If you're not feeling up to that, perhaps you can have your child decorate their desk or school space. You can help them be orderly by showing them where to keep books and markers. Involving your children in the process of creating your "school space" will help them feel loved and special, and it will spark enthusiasm for that first day of school.

❦

In the next chapter, you'll learn how to effectively live out the homeschool life you desire—but first, take action with these getting started steps.

Do you know any homeschoolers in your church or circle of friends that you could connect with? If so, take some time to reach out to them and ask them questions. If not, search the internet or social media for homeschool groups in your area. Then, set some times on your calendar when you will tackle the steps listed in this chapter. Ask your spouse, family member, or friend to mind your children so you can have focused, undistracted time to do this.

As you proceed with your action steps, check off the completed tasks as you go:

- *Complete legal steps*
- *Find community*
- *Choose method*
- *Choose curriculum*
- *Purchase any additional materials needed*
- *Map out the school year*
- *Organize homeschool space*
- *Hire tutor or extra help (if applicable)*

Chapter 6

Living Out Your Homeschool Life

L ife for a homeschool parent is a juggling act, and it can be overwhelming at times, especially when you're just starting out. This chapter is meant to be an "insider's guide" that will show you how to effectively manage your home and school while keeping your cool.

How Do I Maintain Order in My Home?

Clear the clutter!

There's something so refreshing about walking into a well-kept home. My Grandma Edith is a good example of being clean and orderly. From her lovingly manicured garden to her hand-polished tile floors, I feel an air of calm come over me when I step into her beautiful, fresh-smelling, modern home. Of course, she doesn't have little kids running around making messes anymore, but I admire how she keeps everything in its place. It's easy to find what you are looking for in her house because her drawers and cabinets are clutter free. When I asked her how she can keep such a tidy house, she said she'd learned, as she got older, to not keep too many belongings. Having too much stuff actually causes disorder because it's difficult to find homes for all of those things! If it doesn't have any significant value, or hasn't been used in a few months, she will give it away.

Lessons like these have been instrumental to my life and our homeschool because I believe it's important for my children to study in a tidy, organized environment. A cluttered environment causes brain chaos, but an orderly environment creates peace of mind.[xxv] Several studies have proven this. Researchers from Princeton University's Neuroscience Institute conducted a study to understand the brain's responses to both organized and unorganized stimuli. They wanted to see how each environment affects task performance. They published their results in 2011 which showed clearly that clutter is distracting, and it limits one's ability to focus. In an organized environment, the researchers found candidates to be less irritable, more productive, and better able to process information.[xxvi]

The funny thing is, having said all this, you probably assume I'm one of those uber-organized, "type A" personalities. I'm not. I'm . . . whatever the opposite of that is! I wish organization came naturally to me. I love having everything in order, but I struggle to find homes for my belongings and then maintain the order (especially with four busy boys in the house). For example, I bought a birthday card for a friend two months in advance, but I ended up mailing it late because I couldn't find where I put it when it was time to mail it.

Although it's challenging for me to stay organized, homeschooling has given me the drive to work on this area of my life because I desire to have a clean, orderly environment for my family. I have learned valuable lessons throughout the years that have helped me organize my homeschool, so I trust they will help you, too.

The biggest lesson I learned is to take the time to plan. Without a plan in place, your day will be dictated by your children or whatever whim comes your way. If you have a plan to follow, you will be much more focused, efficient, and able to carry out what needs to be done. Just remember that not every day will go as planned—and that's ok. You need to give yourself grace when those uncontrollable interruptions occur, such as a child getting sick or the baby waking up early from a nap.

Also, decide in advance where your homeschool books will go and where you'd like your children to put finished assignments. Choose where their supplies will go so they can follow the system you have created. If *you* don't know where to put their books, how can you expect *your child* to know where to put them when they're finished with them? I also recommend keeping your teaching items in a separate area, such as your planner and assignments that need grading/reviewing

I have learned a lot about organization from several online resources, including flylady.net and blogger/author Crystal Paine. Her blog, moneysavingmom.com, is filled with wisdom for parents.

You'll find excellent tips on topics like how to plan your morning routine and meal plan on a budget. Her blog has links to many free resources and printables for homeschooling. Pinterest.com has creative visual ideas for how to organize your homeschool room. You can look up how to organize a classroom or specific ways of organizing certain objects, like art supplies.

Enlist little helpers

One of the biggest lessons I've had to learn is not to do all the work around the house myself. Gosh—this seems so simple, and yet I struggle with it! Growing up, my mom did the majority of the cleaning in the house, so as an adult I just assumed that it was entirely my responsibility. But when you homeschool, it is nearly impossible to get the house clean BY YOURSELF while also dedicating most of your day to teaching your children.

Recruit your children to help you, and please don't feel guilty about putting them to work. I used to feel this way, because my mom did most everything for me. Occasionally I'd make my bed or fold laundry, but I didn't have any consistent chores. My mom, out of love for me and the desire for a clean house, would tidy my room while I was at school. My bed was always made, floor vacuumed, toys and clothes put neatly away. Although she meant it as a kind gesture, I never learned how to be organized and responsible. It was when I first became a mom and wife that I realized how beneficial it would have been if I had been trained in how to maintain a home. I had to work extra hard to learn how to cook, clean, manage a budget, and other life skills that were now my responsibility.

Learning how to work is one of the most valuable lessons you can give your child. It will prevent fostering a sense of entitlement and they'll grow to appreciate the value and reward of hard work, serving, taking care of themselves, selflessness, cleanliness, and responsibility. Doing chores provides many of the skills needed to prepare them for their future.

Training children takes effort and consistency, but within a relatively short time they will know what is expected of them, and the chores become habit. Initially, it may be frustrating to teach them, but don't give up, because the reward is great. You will have a tidier house, and they will learn valuable skills they'll need for adulthood.

Just tonight, my four-year-old learned a new skill: my husband taught him how to rinse the dishes to prep them for going into the dishwasher. The funny thing is, he resisted by moaning, "But I want to sweep!" We found that hilarious, because it took some time to train him to use the dustpan and broom. When we first taught him, he laid down on the floor in agony over it! But, with persistence and training, it became habit, and at times we would find him sweeping without us asking him to!

The following are some suggested guidelines by age that may help you create realistic expectations for everyone to help around the house.

- *At age 2, a child can help pick up toys. We like to sing "clean up, clean up everybody, everywhere," as we demonstrate how to put the toys away. They can also clean baseboards with a clean wet cloth. We use Norwex microfiber cloths since they are effective for removing bacteria, yet they are completely safe for children and pets.*

- *At age 3, they love to sort, so matching the clean socks or sorting the silverware both work well. Make sure to keep the sharp knives out of reach, though!*

- *At age 4, little ones can sweep, using a dustpan and brush, and help unload the dishwasher. This works best when my two sons work together at this. They call it "the machine," and while one takes the items out of the dishwasher, the other puts them away. They like making sound effects to go along with their "machine," too!*

- *At age 5, kids can use a Dustbuster to vacuum the stairs, and collect plastic recyclables from the house to put in an outdoor bin.*

- *At age 6, you can teach them how to fold towels and sheets. Place the sheet on a clean floor or carpet while you take hold of two corners of the sheet, and your child takes the other two corners. Have them meet you with their corners as you grab them and add them to yours. Then have them reach down and gather the two corners and lift them towards you again, making a second fold.*

- *At age 7, they can vacuum, fold laundry, rake leaves, and wash windows.*

- *At age 8, teach your child to disinfect the bathroom sinks and gather the trash bags from all bathrooms in the house to empty into one large bag for disposal.*

- *At age 9, your child can be responsible for taking care of your pet (including cleaning up after it!). They can also be shown how to do the dishes.*

- *At age 10, kids can maintain a garden, including pulling weeds and watering. They can sort laundry into piles— whites, colors, and delicates, or however your family's sorting system works.*
- *At age 11, your child can learn how to mow the lawn and plunge a toilet.*
- *At age 12, train your adolescent to use an iron and run a load of laundry.*
- *At age 13, your youth can do quite a lot! Hold them responsible for doing their own laundry, cleaning their own room, and whatever chores you decide upon that would be helpful to the family—childcare, edge-trimming the lawn, putting out the garbage, and cleaning the car.*

It's also helpful to train your children to cook a few simple meals, so that they are able to help cook family meals on occasion. They will be better prepared for when they leave the house. Snapping green beans and shucking corn can be great fun for kids of all ages! Some families begin teaching proper knife skills at age 4 or 5—closely supervised!—and others might let their child choose a "signature dish" that they prepare for the family a couple times a month. (One family does something similar as part of each child's 8th birthday milestones!) As the child demonstrates responsibility, they're able to add dishes to their "signature," and by the time they hit double digits they're equipped with the tools to make a full meal for the family. Don't underestimate what your not-so-little one is capable of!

Yes, it takes patience, and you'll have to accept that your six-year-old's way of folding laundry or putting away silverware is not how you would do it; but trust me, it gets easier when you put in the effort to show them how, and it only gets better as they grow older. Think of your home as a business enterprise: you and your spouse are the managers, and your children are your employees. In order for your "business" to run well, there needs to be a plan and proper team instruction. For example, how will the house stay clean if no one knows what job they are responsible for, and when? Or how will they know how to fold the laundry if they haven't been taught? It's important we treat our "employees" fairly and reward the child who is diligent with their chores. Chore charts can work well for motivating the child and helping them to see what is expected of them. You can find chore charts just about everywhere. I like the ones on FlyLady.net, or I create my own.

As you can imagine, enlisting the help of your children is incredibly helpful to keeping order in the home, and for maintaining mom and dad's sanity!

Get extra help when you need it

There will be times where you need some extra help to maintain your home. It could be due to an illness or injury, welcoming a new baby, or a death in the family. I used to shy away from asking for help, not wanting to bother people; I allowed my pride to get in the way. After my fourth C-section, though, I was ready to accept all the help I could get! I had extensive surgery after the birth to remove scar tissue from previous births. I had lost a lot of blood and was very weak. Fortunately, I had an amazing church family step in to offer their help with cleaning, taking care of my children, and bringing us meals. Our immediate families helped as well, but because they lived far from us they were not able to help as much as they would have liked. If you don't have family around to help, plan on having friends or church family help, or ask for recommendations of someone you could hire if needed. You may be able to find other homeschool families with responsible teens who could assist you.

Plan your meals

How will you know what's for dinner tonight without having a plan in place ahead of time?

When I first became a wife, I didn't know what meal planning was. I'd decide that day what we would eat for dinner, which often led to us eating out or needing to go food shopping as soon as my husband got home. Then we'd be eating late dinners, which would set our son's bedtime back too late.

Now I plan my meals usually a week in advance, or, if I'm feeling extra ambitious, a month in advance. This has helped me in a number of ways: my kids are not constantly asking me what's to eat (they look at the menu on the fridge); it helps me to know what we're eating so I make sure we're getting enough balance of healthy foods; I stick to my grocery list which helps me avoid excess spending; and I'm visiting the grocery store a LOT less, which I love.

To do this, you can print or draw a weekly or monthly calendar and pick all your meals for each day. We usually incorporate two vegetarian dishes a week to save money, a fun meal on Fridays for our family fun night, and a leftover-meal day. I make sure to prepare something easy like a crock pot meal on the days I know I'm extra busy.

I also like to incorporate freezer meals into my monthly plan. I double a recipe of something that freezes well so that I have the extra portion ready to take out on days when it's needed. Perhaps we're sick, too tired to cook, or want to bless someone else with a meal. A fun way to prepare freezer meals is to do it together with someone. One time, my friend Erica and I agreed on a few favorite recipes to prepare together. We shopped for the ingredients separately (after we decided who bought what) and then set aside a day to prepare them together. We had fun chatting while meal prepping, and our kids enjoyed a playdate. We made four meals in two hours. Seeing those meals in my freezer was a happy reminder of the fun we had, and they were incredibly helpful to us throughout the month. I highly recommend doing it!

After you have your meal plan in place, set aside time when you can go grocery shopping (preferably by yourself, so you don't have distractions that would slow you down or little ones begging you to purchase foods that are not on your list). In some areas, you can order your groceries online and pick them up at your local grocery store. More and more stores are adopting this tremendously helpful service. A woman I know from our homeschool co-op schedules her grocery order for pickup every Monday afternoon, right after co-op is over, when she and the kids are already in the car. Now that's efficient!

Give yourself grace

We can be our own worst critic. We compare ourselves with others and feel defeated if we don't "match up" to the expectations we've placed on ourselves. If you can relate, may I encourage you to rest in God's promises and give yourself grace?

One area where I have consistently beaten myself up is keeping my house neat. I used to feel discouraged that I couldn't maintain the kind of house my mom did growing up; I remember it consistently being showroom quality. Over the years, I realized that even my type-A homeschool friends were having a hard time keeping their homes consistently tidy. Most of the homeschooling moms I know—myself included!—struggle to keep an orderly house because we're either out of the house, or our house is getting constant use with little people making messes all around us!

I found a cute sign in a Pennsylvania Dutch country store once that read, "Excuse the mess, we're making memories." I love that plaque, because it shows that this is a season in life, and that we shouldn't stress out wondering what people will think if they see a pile of toys on the living room floor. Rather, our hearts should be focused on loving our children, not concentrated on maintaining a perfect-looking house.

I do enjoy having a clean, tidy house, but I've also learned to give myself grace when it's just plain messy. It's perfectly acceptable to have a friend over even if there's a mountain of clean laundry waiting to be folded and dishes in the sink. Having a perfect house doesn't necessarily equate to a person that "has it all together," and having a messy house doesn't invalidate a person's worth, either!

I'm thankful that my husband and I have worked on how to communicate our expectations; for example, I expect him to empty the trash each night, and he expects me to make dinner. Over the years, my husband has grown to understand that since I don't have the house to myself, like I would if our kids were in school, it's nearly impossible to keep the house sparkling clean. He has been incredibly supportive and kind to me during those times when I get down on myself for not being able to "keep up" with everything. There can be mountains of clean laundry piled in our room for days, waiting to be folded, but he is patient, understanding that the job of raising four boys is what is most important.

I hope you have this type of encouragement also. But if not, pray and ask the Lord to fill your heart with joy and purpose, understanding that your worth comes from Him.

Know too, that it is the Lord we are working for—not the praise of men. You can bring glory to God in everything you do. I believe as you pray, God will help you to rejoice in the work you do, even if it seems mundane. The Lord delights in you, and He loves it when you are thankful and desire to be with Him. Psalm 139:17-18 says, "How precious to me are your thoughts, O God! How vast is the sum of them. Were I to count them, they would outnumber the grains of sand."

It helps me to know that I'm not alone in my parenting or in my daily routine as a mom and teacher. I love to hear that the powerful, almighty God cares about the little details of our lives and meets us right where we are. It helps me to remember this when I'm changing diapers for the tenth time that day or when I'm cleaning up milk that just spilled all over my kitchen floor: Jesus is delighting in me.

Your job as a mom can feel insignificant at times. It's messy. Our children can be ungrateful and sometimes unkind. Just remember that Jesus will enable you, through His Spirit, to conquer thoughts of inadequacy and discouragement. Do what you do to the glory of God. He will delight in you, and your children will learn well from watching you!

Making Homeschooling Work on a Tight Budget

If finances are an issue, let me encourage you with my story. As I stated earlier, I was unhappy with my son in public school, but private Christian school was not an option for us financially. Even if we were awarded a scholarship, we still could not have afforded it. My husband was a full-time graduate student, and I was a stay-at-home mom. We were living in section-8 housing, eligible for government assistance, and we didn't have any money to put away into savings, let alone extra money to spend. When I researched education options, I was surprised to find that homeschooling was the most economical option possible, even on our tight budget.

In my first year of homeschooling, I found a free, state-funded, online charter school that provided all of the curriculum, online instruction, materials (including a loaner laptop and printer), and offered field trip opportunities. This was a great way for us to begin homeschooling, especially since we couldn't afford our own computer.

After a year of the online school, we decided to try something different, but we were still in the same financial situation. I asked many homeschool families what curricula they liked best. I ended up piecing together a complete curriculum of used books that others passed down to me.

I also utilized our public library for supplemental resources. One of our local librarians had homeschooled her four children, and she created a display each month with books geared specifically toward homeschoolers. The library also had a binder full of information for homeschoolers, including a list of the local homeschool co-ops. This may be something your library has, too.

Homeschool co-ops are an affordable way to provide your child access to classes you'd prefer to outsource. I have been part of several different co-ops that were either no cost or minimal cost. In one co-op, the parents took turns teaching, while in another, the same parent taught a subject for a given length of time, usually a quarter. My children made great friends and participated in a range of different group lessons like public speaking, performance, physical education, and science. One co-op even had volunteers from the church to watch the babies in the nursery.

Co-ops are a cost-effective way for your children to receive lessons, compared to the high price tag of a tutor or specialized class. Through co-ops and other homeschool groups, you'll meet many parents with whom you could share curricula or swap books. One of my homeschool-mom friends hosted a curriculum swap at her home, where we could bring the books we were no longer using and swap them for any books offered.

Another way I've saved money on homeschooling is through the internet. The internet can be a useful tool for finding free educational resources. For example, my brother gave my son his old trumpet, but private lessons were too expensive for us. I looked online and found a series of trumpet lessons for free on the YouTube channel called "learnitonlinetoday." He picked it up quickly, and I'm thankful that we had it at the ready when his interest was piqued. My other son wanted to learn how to draw a dragon, so I looked online and discovered artforkidshub.com, a site that has a series of complimentary videos teaching kids how to draw various things, including dragons. He enjoyed following along to the video and produced a highly detailed piece by the end of it! I've also used free printable resources and created my own crossword puzzles online (puzzle-maker.com/CW) for my boys, inserting their vocabulary words. Similarly, there are sites where you can make personalized handwriting sheets (like handwritingworksheets.com). There are even large-scale curriculum helps, too. A completely free "all in one" Christian homeschool curriculum exists at allinonehomeschool.com. It was created by a mother of six who wanted to document lessons for her children while providing easy lesson plans for homeschooling parents.

Take advantage of what the community has to offer. My oldest son had the privilege of learning chemistry in 5th grade from a retired chemistry teacher who had access to the high school science lab. The classes were excellent and were completely free for homeschoolers! A single-mom friend of mine who homeschools her two teenage sons has them take affordable violin lessons from an older lady; her sons have experience performing for the community through a free homeschool orchestra led by a professional conductor who had homeschooled her four children. A homeschool dad I know enrolled his two sons in a highly-praised community children's choir. Several of my friends have their children take art lessons from the university near them. The lessons are taught by college art education students who need to gain experience teaching, so the lessons are high quality, yet very affordable.

Some performance venues will offer deep discounts to their matinee shows for homeschoolers. My children have been exposed to a vast array of professional performances because of this, including African drummers, Chinese dancers, Cirque du Soleil acrobats, and on-stage versions of TV shows such as *Odd Squad*.

As your children get older, you can have them raise part of the money needed to go on a youth group retreat or other experience they want to participate in. Not only will that help you financially, but it will teach them that things in life don't come easy or free. They will have a sense of accomplishment and gratitude if they helped to earn it.

Homeschooling with a Baby

Having a baby in the house presents an added challenge when homeschooling, but also an abundance of joy! As I'm writing this, my youngest just turned one, and my older sons adore the time they get to spend with their littlest brother during the day. They think he's cute and are often entertained by his adorable ways. He brings a happy presence to our home classroom as he delights in what his older brothers are doing.

I'm thankful for this perspective, since again, I came from a background where I didn't like to babysit, was a mother before I was ready, and couldn't imagine teaching more than one child at a time. I never would have guessed I'd be where I am now. As it turned out, I have had two babies while homeschooling, and managed to keep up with it even through C-section births.

Recovering from those surgeries was the most difficult part of teaching my children at home, yet at the same time it was marvelously helpful. My oldest attended to my younger ones while I rested, and he learned how to serve by helping me. Years after that experience, he still surprises me on occasion by making me tea and placing it on a table by the couch so I can rest!

Something that helped me during those early days with a newborn was to take time off from teaching. I planned the school year to start a month early so I could take that month to recover. I also asked for help in advance. I knew I would need help making meals, cleaning, and caring for my older children. Friends and church members kindly agreed to help during my recovery. With my fourth-born, I was able to find a young lady that was homeschooled to come a few times a week to help teach my children. That was a huge blessing!

If you are in that stage where you are recovering from birth, and waking up through the night, please don't be afraid to request help. I know how hard it can be to ask for assistance, as I lived miles away from my parents and had a hard time asking others for help. I have learned, though, that often what I thought would be a huge inconvenience for someone actually turned out to be a blessing for them. For example, my neighbor had our sons over to play while I napped, and she said having them over actually helped her to get work done in her house—her children weren't vying for her attention because they were happily playing with mine. So, reach out when you need it, and pray God provides just the right people to help.

Once I healed and got back to homeschooling on my own, my regularly planned schedule needed to be revised according to the baby's nap times. In those early months, I needed my rest from being up through the night with the baby, so my husband would take the "morning shift" before going off to graduate school. Throughout the day, I utilized baby's nap times as prime teaching time. When baby was awake, I would give the older children independent work or allow them to watch an educational show. Often, I held the baby in a carrier so I could have my hands free to instruct. For the first year of my baby's life he was generally content to be held in the baby carrier for a good part of the day. He loved being close to me, hearing my voice, and watching what I was doing. If he got cranky, I'd go down the checklist in my mind (is he hungry, tired, changed, too hot/cold?), and if it was none of the typical causes, it was either because he was ill, teething, or needing stimulation. Stimulation isn't usually a problem for my youngest with having three older brothers running around, but it's something to consider. If your baby needs stimulation, consider getting him board books and toys that he can have at certain times of the day when you need him to be occupied. Also, allow him to sit in a high chair and watch while you are doing your science experiments or cooking meals. Babies are curious explorers, wanting to learn and experience new things daily. My baby loved sitting in a Bumbo seat or high chair near us while we did art projects, listened to memory work on CDs, or conducted science experiments.

Furthermore, my babies all enjoyed being outside, and this is my go-to for calming a fussy baby. If it's a nice day out, I love to bring our schoolroom outside, and the baby can be with us in the carrier, stroller, or swing. The stimulation of birds singing, butterflies fluttering, and flowers to smell often soothed him and sometimes lulled him to sleep.

Something I've learned, after having four boys, is that babies CAN learn self-control after about 8 months old. I know, it sounds funny, but it's true! I have the baby on a routine, and the routine means he knows what to expect—and when we both know what to expect, it helps our day to go more smoothly. For example, I know that the baby will go down for his nap at 11am, so the older ones benefit from prime teaching time, and the baby thrives on having a consistent nap schedule. When the baby wakes again, I make sure his needs are met, and I give him some one-on-one play time. Afterwards, I sit him in a gated, baby-proofed play area. When I first started put him in there, he cried after I walked away, but after only a few minutes he happily entertained himself. Each time I did this, he would fuss less because he grew accustomed to the routine.

This exercise not only will help you to accomplish tasks, but you are teaching your baby the vital skill of self-control.

I find the toddler years to be more difficult to manage during school time because they are often into mischief. You may be teaching a math lesson in one room and find out your toddler has been unraveling all the toilet paper in the other room. Potty training takes up a lot of time, as does training in obedience. Toddlers need lots of attention; but what I have learned is that teaching them to patiently wait (in small increments, gradually working your way to more time) is healthy for them. If you simply turn on the TV every time you need to give the older ones attention, they will not learn the necessary character trait of self-control. However, I advise you to give your youngest child attention first, then work with your next youngest child, and work your way upwards in age.

Once the little ones' needs are met and they have a good fill of mommy time, they are ready to play independently. Prepare a basket filled with toys that the young ones can play with only at a designated time. That way, these will be special in your child's eyes, and it will keep them busy. You can also have your preschooler sit in a high chair and offer a snack to eat or a craft to do. Involve your toddler in projects when you're able. Toddlers love to be included in music and nature exploration. You could also find a trustworthy homeschooled high schooler (because they can be available during the day) to come over a couple times a week to play with the younger ones while you spend time lesson planning or teaching the older ones. And, of course, utilize those nap times either for instruction time or a mommy "time-out."

Teaching Multiple Grade Levels

Initially, the thought of teaching all my children (who are not close in age) seemed a daunting task. I didn't understand how people could teach kindergarten, middle school, and high school simultaneously. After observing several large homeschool families over the years, I discovered that there are advantages to children learning in a group of multiple ages. For one, students are all advancing in their studies and growing together. They learn how to hold their own as they relate intellectually with various ages and abilities.

In many ways, homeschooling multiple children is reminiscent of the educational style of a one-room schoolhouse. Before the 1920s, American children attended school in these one-room setups consisting of rows of desks where children of various ages were taught in the same classroom. The students would progress at their own rate for reading, grammar, and math. All the other subjects could be taught as a group: spelling, geography, history, science, art, PE, and music. Students could all learn about the Renaissance period while writing or drawing about it according to their ability level.

Children advanced in their studies not only from being taught by the teacher, but through learning from the older students. The teacher would have the older students help teach as part of their education. This process reinforced the older students' learning and benefitted the younger students. If you have multiple children, you'll notice that the younger ones naturally look up to the older ones, often imitating them.

Contrary to what one might think, these one-room schoolhouses were not chaotic. The teacher commanded respect and had the authority to discipline if a child was unruly (just as you do as parent). Because of this, children were more likely to be good listeners and follow the rules of the classroom.

Children were accustomed to hard work and were expected to help the teacher. The older students were responsible for bringing in water and carrying in coal or wood for the stove. The younger students were given responsibilities according to their size and ability such as cleaning the blackboard/chalkboard and taking the erasers outside for dusting.

As home educators, we can learn a lot from the ways of the one-room schoolhouse model to apply to our own homes, don't you think? One aspect I implement from this approach is having my older children teach the younger ones to solidify their own studies. Many curriculum providers specialize in creating material suitable for teaching multiple levels, such as My Father's World, Sonlight, or Heart of Dakota. It will also save you both time and money to purchase one curriculum package with separate workbooks for each child rather than a completely separate curriculum for each child. If you have specific questions regarding how to use one curriculum for multiple children, many homeschool publishers will offer free consultations with advisors via phone, email, or even live chat.

The Classical Conversations group we've been a part of models an inclusive system for K-6th where multiple age groups learn the same material, yet at a level appropriate to their ability. For example, all students are asked to memorize a poem to present before the class, yet the expectations for each child varies by age. The Kindergartners may recite a poem with one stanza, and they are applauded for the practice of public speaking alone. The 6th graders may memorize a poem with five stanzas, and are expected to stand up straight, look at their audience, use hand gestures, and project their voice.

In my home, I am currently teaching grades pre-K, 2nd, and 8th. A typical school day for us begins after the kids have helped to clean the kitchen after breakfast. They know that we are to meet at the table, pray, do a short devotional, and discuss the day's lessons. Then my oldest gets started on an assignment from his math tutor while I teach math to the younger ones. My preschooler loves to do what my 2nd grader is doing, so he joins in with his own math book, and—to my surprise!—he has caught on very quickly and is doing first grade math! During this time, the baby is in the room with us, playing with "special" toys reserved just for these learning times. After math, I set up my middle two with a hands-on activity or craft while I put the baby down for a nap and check on my oldest. I make sure he has done his work and answer any questions he has. For the most part, he works independently. He likes being a self-paced learner, and I'm grateful he is learning how to manage his time and meet deadlines, like turning in his language arts papers on Fridays. The baby generally naps for a good three hours, and in that time I am able to complete the lessons for the day with my middle two sons. My oldest will join in with them for science experiments, occasional history studies, art and enrichment activities like woodworking and field trips. In the evenings, when my husband is home, the kids like to share a highlight from the day or relate something they've learned. Sometimes my husband will come prepared with something to teach them. One time he brought a large lens to the dinner table and taught them about refraction.

How we conduct school will inevitably vary from your schedule, especially depending on the season of life you're in. However, the system of allowing the learning to trickle down from oldest to youngest can still remain the same. In my household, I've been amazed at the educational growth of my preschooler because of what he has picked up from his older siblings. As your children progress, they will increasingly be more independent and responsible. The goal is to have children who love to learn, and who take charge of their own education. Self-teaching is an extremely valuable skill that will make them stand out among their peers at college and on into adulthood.

Keeping Your Child Physically Active

You'll be happy to learn that there are many options for your child to develop athletically while homeschooling. Homeschooling provides the freedom and flexibility necessary for athletes to practice at various hours. Even if your child does not want to be the next pro-BMX biker or star gymnast, you'll find many ways to get your child involved in healthy activity. There are plenty of community resources that provide athletics for homeschooled students, including the YMCA and Upward Sports. Check with local specialty centers like dance, gymnastics, skating, etc.; these frequently offer sports classes specifically for homeschoolers. (We found a nearby skiing center in Pennsylvania with discounted daytime classes.) There are also many co-ops that have physical education class.

In the younger years, you can do simple things like taking your child hiking, playing running games in the backyard like "red light, green light," and creating obstacle courses in your basement. You can teach your daughter or son how to jump rope and play double-dutch. They can ride their bike, go sledding, or work out to an exercise video for kids.

As your child gets older, team sports are beneficial in a number of ways. Your child will learn how to be a team player, follow directions, gain confidence, develop respect for authority figures (coaches), and build friendships. It will also provide them with consistent physical exercise, and you may discover your child's potential for excelling in a particular sport that could lead to scholarships for college or even playing professionally.

Professional athlete Tim Tebow benefitted from being allowed to play football for his local high school team when he was homeschooled. According to Tim Tebow's mother, Pam,

> *"It has been my experience that the families who homeschool are a positive addition to an athletic team, school band, or interest club. Parents are usually involved and are willing to volunteer to assist the various programs. The character of the homeschooled students is often an encouragement to those in their sphere of influence. All five of our children were educated*

at home, and all of them received scholarships to college: academic, music, and athletic. Some of them would not have received scholarships if they had been prohibited from participating in extracurricular activities at our local school."[xxvii]

Travel teams are another option for developing athletic skills in various sports. In 6th and 7th grade, our son participated in our community's soccer travel league which had a mix of public-schooled and homeschooled boys in it. Our son loved being part of the team comradery, and it fulfilled his need to be active. He discovered his natural athletic abilities and areas that needed more practice. It also created bonding experiences for our family when we came to cheer him on during games.

For the gifted child who wants to become a professional athlete, homeschooling allows them the time to train diligently and study topics pertinent to that concentration, such as nutrition and physiology. Serena Williams and her sister, Venus, were both ranked #1 tennis stars in the world during their career, and they were both homeschooled by their father, Richard. He chose to homeschool so they'd have time to focus on their sport. Other professional athletes who were homeschooled include Blake Griffin, professional basketball player for the Detroit Pistons (NBA); Simone Biles, three-time gymnastics world champion and 2016 Olympic all-around champion; Steele Johnson, Olympic medalist for diving; and professional surfer Bethany Hamilton. Bethany says of her homeschool experience, "It makes it easier to be a career surfer and to travel. My mom is my teacher and I get a lot of my assignments online. Typically, my workload is just like that of a public high school student with the exception that I can do it on my hours. A lot of my friends are homeschooled as well, so we end up having the same schedule of surfing, traveling, and then homework."[xxviii]

Nurturing Your Marriage

For some reason, it seems common in our society for parents to give their all to their children while sacrificing their marriage relationship. May I plead with you not to put your relationship on hold while you wait for your children to grow up? I have been advised of this by many a wise older woman. It's too easy to get caught up in the demands of the household and become completely exhausted without leaving any part of you left for your spouse.

An older woman I knew spoke to my heart when she told me about a simple practice she and her husband did to prioritize their relationship. When her husband came home from work, he greeted the kids, kissed her, and then they'd sit on the couch and discuss their day. By doing this, they demonstrated their commitment of love, connected by communicating, and set an example for their children of how important the marriage relationship is. The children also learned to respect their parents' time by being taught not to interrupt. They didn't like it at first, but over time it brought them peace and stability; as adults, they remember how mommy and daddy loved each other enough to give each other the gift of time. My husband and I don't always do this, but I've found on the days that we do, there's less room for miscommunication, and we feel more connected and in love. I encourage you to try it! The evening hours are a busy time of day, but if you could take just fifteen minutes to do this with your spouse each day, it will make a difference in your relationship. You (and your spouse) are worth it!

Just as you can plan your lessons, outings, and your meals, make sure planning dates is up there on your to-do list. Put them on your calendar. The times I don't intentionally schedule a date night, I'm amazed down the road at how many weeks have slipped away since the last time I had a date with my spouse. Going on dates shouldn't be seen as selfish or reserved for only special occasions; rather, they should be a regular part of your routine so that your marriage will flourish. A healthy marriage will create a healthy family, providing stability for the home environment. I know, for myself, when I spend time with my spouse away from the kids, it reminds me of who I am outside of "mom." My husband and I typically feel re-energized and, again, more united.

A quick word of advice: don't expect your spouse to plan the dates. Go ahead and get the OK to put some dates on the calendar—then YOU make it happen. If finances are an issue or you can't find a babysitter, plan a date at home; you can put the kids to bed early, or put on a special movie on for them, while you do something in another room. If you want to get out, find a family to swap babysitting with, or ask an older couple from church who may love the opportunity to spend some time with your children, especially if you do not have family nearby. There are also several options in many communities that offer parents' night out events; check local churches, Bricks4Kidz, gyms, and the YMCA.

Be Good to Yourself!

As a homeschool parent, you'll have to be intentional about giving yourself time. Your days are full of endless tasks, and it's paramount to understand that your well-being also needs attention. Your health is necessary to run your house well. By "health," I mean you must consider the spiritual, physical, and emotional aspects of your being.

First, it's vital that we fill our tank with God's Spirit rather than risking "running on fumes" for the day. The true source of my strength and my patience comes from above, and if I'm not communing with the Lord, I notice (as do my children) just how irritable I can be. As a Christian, I seek to have time each day where I'm reading my Bible, praying, and listening. For me, I typically pray while in the shower (where it's quiet!), lead a devotional with my boys after breakfast, and then spend my personal time with the Lord just after I put the baby down for a nap. There are so many other things I can be doing during baby's nap, but as the saying goes, "I'm too busy not to pray!" When I make the time for Him, He always blesses it and gives me the calm I need for the day. I take about 15-20 minutes, sitting in our screened-in porch overlooking the flowers, to pray and read my Bible while my four-, seven-, and thirteen-year-olds are busy doing independent workbooks at the kitchen table.

You must also work in how you will exercise and manage healthy living habits, such as a regular bedtime and eating well. I find that when I take the time to exercise, it increases my energy, and I feel much happier. You don't need a gym to get a healthy amount of exercise into your day. I like to walk around the neighborhood with the baby in the stroller while my older boys ride their bikes. If we have to be indoors, I will jump on my mini-trampoline, do circuits with the boys, dance to the radio—and, of course, I am running up and down stairs all day long! I have also participated in Zumba, Fitness Inspired classes (livefitnessinspired .com), and an indoor soccer league. (Note: I did not do them all at once. These are just examples to give you ideas.)

Going to bed at a reasonable hour is one of my biggest struggles, because I enjoy the quiet of night and being able to accomplish what I could not during the day. Yet, I always regret staying up too late. You can never get those lost hours of sleep back, even if you are able to nap during the day. To be your best self for teaching your children and living life, be sure to get at least seven hours of sleep at night. (This is, of course, speaking to when you have that option. Many of us are up during the night with babies). Having proper rest will make you more alert, emotionally stable, and give you a healthier body.

Your emotional health is crucial to having a healthy functioning home. When you are upset, the whole house feels it, right? Yet when you are optimistic, you feel more controlled, and your family benefits from it. Knowing what your triggers are will help you to avoid feeling burned out. I know that I am an introvert, and at times I crave my personal space. I bought a shirt with the NASA logo on it that made me laugh. It reads: "I need my space." I can relate to that in more than one way! I know I need time to myself to process my thoughts and rest. Without it, I feel stressed, worn out, and I quickly lose patience. So, I try to make it a point to have at least thirty minutes to myself every day, and right now I schedule that around the baby's nap. I start with my Bible time and write in my journal; then I read, take a power nap, or check my email. I've trained my children to be quiet when baby's napping, and when my door is closed, it means "Do not disturb! (Unless there's an emergency!)" Perhaps you're an extrovert and time connecting with your friends is necessary. Make time to call them, or get together while your kids play. Know what you need, and make it a point to make it happen.

I highly recommend openly informing your partner about your needs *before* it's urgent, if possible. Talk with your spouse about scheduling times on the calendar for them to watch the kids while you go out, or vice versa—they take the kids out of the house while you have it to yourself. I have been guilty of not communicating my needs properly and assuming my husband knows what I need when I need it—without talking to him. He should just KNOW, right?! Wrong. I have learned that clear communication of expectations is key. It will prevent discord and give you both what you need. You can press on, knowing you have time scheduled to look forward to and get refreshed!

Live it Out

After reading this chapter, which of the topics do you project will be the hardest for you to live out? I encourage you to take note of what you learned and proactively determine to achieve a healthy balance in those areas. For example, do you need to set a date on the calendar to have a family clean-up day so the cleaning burden is not all on you? Or do you need to spend some time preparing some activities for your baby to engage with during school hours? Whatever it is, take note of it now, and make sure to schedule a time to do it.

When you're finished, reward yourself. Go on, you deserve it! Treat yourself to an ice cream cone, take a bubble bath, or sit back and watch your favorite show. Or, treat yourself to finishing this book . . .!

Chapter 7

Home: Your Mission Field

Do you ever feel like, as a mom, you aren't doing enough to help others? I do—especially when I read about how many people are suffering around the world. One day, while contemplating this, God pressed it upon my heart that, at this point in my life, *my children* are my mission field. He lovingly helped me to see just how important my role is in discipling my children to bear "good fruit," and that this is the will of God for my life right now.

I believe, as Christian parents, we can tend to think we are "not doing enough" for the Lord unless we're out on the mission field or volunteering for many roles in the church. It's important, even if there is a need, that we seek the Lord's will before committing to serving others. Even though it's good work, it may not be what God has called you to at this season in your life. If it is preventing you from the time needed to effectively teach and train your children, it may not be your time to serve.

Lisa Terkeurst's book *The Best Yes* has helped me learn to pray first before committing my time and energy to someone who asks me to help. Instinctively, I jump to say yes, but what I realized after reading that book is that not every "yes" I have made has been one God intended for me. I remember one year I had said "yes" to too many people, and I was completely worn out. I wanted to help, but it was unrealistic for me to take on as much as I did. With a new baby, I helped lead a children's ministry, took on a leadership role at MOPS, agreed to join the choir, played piano during services at church, and homeschooled my boys during the day. A few months into juggling all of this, I ended up in the hospital. My immune system was weak, since I was not getting good rest at night and had worn myself too thin helping others—even though I truly loved each thing I was involved with. My family suffered too, as they received less of my attention. Choosing the "best yes," as Lisa says, can apply to our homeschools, too. Make sure that what you are teaching, and what you are committing to outside the home, is going to be in line with what God wants for you at this time. Over-commitment can lead to fatigue, impatience, and not enough time to properly train your children.

In the timeline of life, we have a very short window of opportunity to teach our children. We are raising up disciples, and it is through a committed, undistracted labor of love that we will reap an eternal reward.

Incorporating Bible study

A unique privilege God has given us parents is to "train a child in the way he should go" (Proverbs 22:6 ESV). According to the Bible (Deuteronomy 11:19), we are to talk about Him to our children when we rise and when we lie down. In our own family, we begin and end our day with Bible time, and we pray or have discussions about the Lord throughout the day—just another perk of having them at home.

We have incorporated different ways of spending time with the Lord. Sometimes I have the kids gather around the piano while we sing a hymn (and my toddler loves to participate by enthusiastically shaking a maraca!). Other times we will read a Bible verse and discuss how it can be applied to our lives. Most recently, we have been using my seven- and four-year-olds' AWANA books to memorize scripture and study God's Word, while my thirteen-year-old reads his Bible and devotion book on his own. Then we join in prayer together for the day. Starting our day with devotions sets the tone for the day. We are acknowledging God as a priority in our lives and allowing His Spirit to work in us.

Let me pause here for a minute to tell you that it is perfectly normal to have interruptions to your ideal plans, especially when it comes to Bible study. The Enemy does not want us teaching our children to be obedient to God's word, and often that resistance comes in the form of our children's behavior. Honestly, there have been days I had to put myself in time-out in the middle of devotion time to go vent to God in my room: "I don't understand, God! I'm

145

starting our day with prayer and trying my best to lead my children to You, but they won't cooperate! You have to help me!" With parenting in general, we will have times where we just want to throw in the towel; it's certainly not exclusive to homeschooling. Yet God gives us this promise: "Let us not become weary in doing good, for at the proper time we will reap a harvest if we do not give up" (Galatians. 6:9).

Try not to let the Enemy steal your joy. Instead, as calmly as possible, take the appropriate disciplinary action, and resume with the lesson. For example, during a time of Bible reading, two of my boys kept poking each other. I had to separate them, putting one child on either side of me, so they would be quiet and not annoy each other. Another time my one child was smirking and making faces at my other child, causing him to giggle and interrupt. I had that child leave the room and he had to do that lesson on his own after his time out. These are just some examples, but the main thing is to keep pointing them to Jesus. We are all in need of a Savior, and by frequently incorporating Bible instruction into your day, having your children memorize Scripture, and setting the example of asking the Lord for forgiveness when we sin, they, too, will come to understand why they need Him, allowing the Holy Spirit to mold their character into Christ-likeness.

Discovering Your Child's Kingdom Purpose and Identifying Their Spiritual Gifts

Our children have a call on their lives to fulfill a specific kingdom purpose. It was placed in them before they were born. King David recognized this in Psalm 139:15-16:

> *My frame was not hidden from you*
> *when I was made in the secret place,*
> *when I was woven together in the depths of the earth.*
> *Your eyes saw my unformed body;*
> *all the days ordained for me were written in your book*
> *before one of them came to be.*

As parents, we're to intentionally help guide our children to find their calling, and it's up to us to ask the Lord for discernment. A benefit of homeschooling is that you will have ample time to observe your child in various situations. This will help you identify what your child's giftings are. You'll notice their skills and their passions, two indicators that will help you discern their spiritual gifts and God's leading on their life.

Romans 12:6 says, "We have different gifts, according to the grace given to each of us." Besides natural talent and passions, God gives spiritual gifts to those who follow Him, as described in Romans 12:7-8; Ephesians 4:11; and 1 Corinthians 12:6-10. Make sure to allow your child to take part in different activities that will help them see for themselves what God is enabling them to do, and where a trusted mentor can help point out their strengths.

If you don't already know this about yourself, find out what your spiritual gifts are. There are online surveys available to help you discover your gifts at links like spiritualgiftstest.com/tests. Ask the Lord how you can use these gifts, whether you're strongest in one area or you're a bit more multi-faceted. When you serve using your spiritual gift, you will be more fulfilled and better able to serve those around you. The Lord teaches in 1 Peter 4:10, "Each of you should use whatever gift you have received to serve others, as faithful stewards of God's grace in its various forms."

Serving the Community

Earlier, I mentioned that your home is your mission field. Your family should always come first, but there is a time for helping others. God will show you when there is a need He would like you to fill as a family.

Part of training our children as disciples of Jesus is to show them how to care for the needs of others. Through involving your children in community service, you are teaching them to value others ahead of themselves. Because of sin, children are born selfish. Just think of how little they are when they shout, "Mine!" when they don't want to share a toy. Children need help learning how to care for others, which also allows them to practice using the spiritual gifts God has given them. If your child is musically gifted, for example, they may be asked to help lead a church worship service.

When you homeschool, you can make service part of your school schedule, or you can pick a time on the weekend. In our family, we set aside time Sunday after church to help or care for others. It has helped us to have this weekly routine so we don't forget to think about how we can minister to others.

I encourage you to find something your family can do together to serve. It's a win-win-win situation! You'll enjoy a great family bonding experience while teaching the value of service and benefit those who are receiving your service. Some ideas include helping an elderly neighbor, visiting your local nursing home, sorting baby clothes at your local pregnancy resource clinic, preparing gift boxes to go to sick children in the hospital, or mailing handwritten letters.

One of my family's favorite service projects is Operation Christmas Child through Samaritan's Purse. Every year, local groups or individuals collect shoeboxes filled with gifts for overseas children in need. My family has participated in this every year since my oldest was in preschool. Last year, my son was old enough to help at one of the collection centers. There, he spent the better part of two full days of receiving deliveries of shoeboxes from across the US which were then packed and loaded to be shipped overseas.

Another service our family has done together is to through Compassion International and Food for the Hungry. We have two children in Rwanda that we support. Our monthly giving helps provide them with food, clothing, an education, biblical studies, and medical care. My children pray for our sponsored children each night at dinner and occasionally write notes and draw pictures for them. They have received notes in return, which makes the experience more real to them.

We've have had a few entertaining things happen during our days of service. This is to be expected when you bring small children with you, I suppose, but as parents, we can never be quite sure what will happen, right? While in the moment it can be embarrassing, remember: these moments make great stories, and you'll be laughing about it someday! Like the day we visited a nursing home for Christmas. We had finished caroling as a group, and I was looking around for my oldest son. When I found him, he was surrounded by gray heads all looking up at him from their wheelchairs, laughing. He decided to do handstands for them, and they loved it! The nurses told me, "You can leave him here!" Another time, we paired up with my brother-in-law's family. We took the day to perform music at a nursing home. We sang songs, played instruments, danced, and made hand-written notes for the elderly. What we didn't plan for was my eight-year-old son going up to each resident, asking if they wanted his autograph!

It will take some effort (and sometimes courage) to get your children involved in service projects, but it is worth it. By doing so you'll inspire them to be servant leaders and create some wonderful (and perhaps funny) memories to last a lifetime.

Create Your Own School

While homeschooling, you are teaching, discovering, mentoring, nurturing, comforting, and playing with your child. Home educating is a way of life, and it should not be seen as school that is separate from everything else. I think those of us who were educated in a traditional school can tend to take a brick-and-mortar approach. I know I used to. I stressed out if my son didn't complete a worksheet in the thirty minutes I allocated for math, and I made sure we covered every single page of the text we were using. Now, however, I understand that it's perfectly acceptable to jump ahead or only use certain pages of a particular book, as long as my student has a solid grasp of the material. I used to think I wasn't doing a good job of teaching when my son was finished with his work by lunch! I didn't account for all the extra time that is needed in schools just to manage large groups of children. Now I realize that most homeschool children who start in the morning are finished by noon, especially in the younger years—and since so many are demonstrating high scores on national exams, I no longer worry.

It's important to remember that, although you are educating your children and you want them to do well, it's equally fundamental to produce fun memories in the process. You are not a traditional school, so have fun creating *your* ideal school! You can make up your own holidays and traditions that your children will look forward to celebrating together. We take a day off to celebrate the 100th day of school. This is pretty much mid-year, and we like to invite our homeschool friends over for pizza and playtime. My aunt who homeschooled always began their school year with an exciting field trip. A homeschool dad I know started a fun tradition of giving his boys a couple of "golden tickets" at the beginning of the school year. These tickets could be turned in at any time of the year to redeem a day off from school!

Homeschooling is a shared learning experience, so again, make sure it's something you enjoy also. Your children will feed off of your enthusiasm. Understanding takes place by several means, so remember you're not limited to your textbooks. Allow your homeschool materials to work for you, rather than you being enslaved to them. The most meaningful learning experiences I've had are the ones that have been hands-on, so whenever possible, I engage my children in being an active participant in their learning rather than a student that is lectured to all day. I ask them questions like, "How does that make you feel?" "What would you do if you were in that scenario?" "Why do you think that happened?" When teaching my child to memorize a piece, I have them physically walk from room to room as they repeat their stanzas. Then when they have to repeat their verse from memory they will imagine being in those rooms to recall the information. This is based on an old Greek method called *loci*.

I also enjoy showing them how something works rather than simply telling them about it. For example, when we studied ancient Egypt, we read about their language, then wrote our names in hieroglyphics on clay slabs. We learned about a holiday in their culture where they grew lentils, so you can guess what we grew! (Those are fun to grow by the way, since they spout very quickly!)

Creating your school should be a natural extension of how you want your family to live, grow, act, serve, and be. A way to focus your energy on what you value most is to create a motto for your homeschool. Many institutions have them, so why not yours? I've already mentioned the motto of Classical Conversations: "To know God and make Him known." This establishes in a nutshell what this community is all about, helps the tutors not to lose sight of their vision, and helps those under its system to be guided by it.

God has blessed you with your children and given you the unique ability to inspire growth in them. Your unconditional love for your child will push you to teach well, and it motivates them to learn well. You are incredibly important and valued in their eyes. Never forget that. Your child looks up to you and seeks your acceptance and praise. Make sure to make the most of every opportunity to love your child well and, with God's help, to ensure a vibrant, joyful, and encouraging atmosphere for them to develop.

1 Corinthians 15:58 says, "Always give yourselves fully to the work of the Lord, because you know that your labor in the Lord is not in vain." You are on a mission to raise up your children to be the best that they can be for God's glory, so do it with all your might, knowing that it is for a greater purpose with an eternal reward.

ↄ

Putting the "Puzzle Pieces" Together

In the next chapter, you'll get to "meet" real people that have committed themselves fully to educating their children from home. Before I introduce you though, consider the questions below, and then when you're ready, combine your notes from the end of each chapter. This is where you will see the pieces coming together like a puzzle to create a vivid picture of what your homeschool will look like. Reviewing these notes will give you a sense of accomplishment for all you've done, help you remember what you've learned, and will be a visual aid you can keep with you in your organizer to help guide you as you set your homeschool plans.

- *How do you feel about your home as your mission field?*
- *Is there an area of your life where you are over-committed? Or is there a need that God has placed on your heart to fulfill?*
- *Would you like to serve alongside your child in some capacity?*
- *How can you help your child's faith to mature?*
- *Are there new traditions you'd like to start for your family?*

Make sure to discuss these questions with your spouse, if you have one, and list any ideas you have for putting these elements into practice.

Chapter 8

Testimonials

I am incredibly thankful to the people who have submitted their responses to my questions for inclusion in this chapter. Here's where you get to "talk" to people who have been there, done that! You'll meet a wide variety of homeschool parents and pupils to learn from and relate to. Some of these individuals are currently homeschooling, some have homeschooled in the past, and some were homeschooled as a child; here, they have openly shared their experiences with you.

I admire each one of them greatly and know that you will enjoy hearing of their adventures with homeschooling. Most of these people I have known for years and have had the privilege of doing life together—sharing homeschool books, meeting for lunchtime playdates at Chick-Fil-A, chatting late at night about the frustrations during the day. We pray for each other and have celebrated the 100th day of school together (one year with a 100-eyed-creature cookie cake). We swap babysitting sessions, host Chinese students as a group, and experience field trips together (sometimes traveling together to another state). They have seen me at my best and at my worst and have extended their love and grace to me. They have given me tremendous support and wisdom that's helped me persevere with homeschooling my children.

My prayer for you is that you will be filled with the Holy Spirit to discern what God is calling you to do, that you will find uplifting community, and that the testimonials below will give you the encouragement you need. Each person who has shared below is not perfect, but in my mind they are incredibly strong because they have allowed Jesus to work through them to accomplish great things for His glory! They have disciplined themselves to push through the difficulties life brings and rise up above the challenges to do what they believe is best for their children. I also admire the formerly-homeschooled adults who shared; their stories of what life was like as a homeschooled child is insightful and I know you'll enjoy reading their accounts as well.

So, without further ado, I present to you my friends.

∾

Jim and Karen Galambos

Program manager for DARPA (Jim); veteran homeschool parents (5 Years)

"You're not going to be one of *them*, are you?" That was my mother's response when I told her I wanted to homeschool my 5th and 6th graders starting the next fall. She had recently retired from the public school system and felt the same way my father-in-law did. He was also a former teacher and a coach. Needless to say, the hardest part of starting our homeschooling journey was convincing the grandparents that their grandchildren weren't going to receive a second-class education and become social aberrations.

We raised our family in Fairfax County, VA, ranked one of the top five school districts in the nation. Our daughter, Jana, participated in a Spanish immersion program where she learned math and science in Spanish half the day. Our son, Sam, went to a center for gifted children and was considered a bright math mind. Both of the children had friends and participated in community activities. It sounds like an ideal suburban life. But the reality was a bit different. As an adult, when asked who she was as a child, Jana says, "I was continually stressed out. I was in leadership roles such as patrol, honor choir, GT and student council. All I did was work and worry about getting behind in my schoolwork when I got pulled out for one of my 'specials.'" She was having stomach aches every evening and was often up past bedtime doing homework.

My son's experience was somewhat different. At a center for gifted children, everything came with a level of privilege. In fourth grade, his teacher believed in allowing gifted children to pursue their own interests. That was fine in my book, but academic rigor was the sacrifice. The children learned Virginia history the week before the Virginia Standards of Learning (SOL) exam. Most 4th grade students spent the entire year learning Virginia history, but because the kids at the center were "so brilliant," they could quickly learn, recall, and regurgitate Virginia history well enough to pass the SOL. So, they did just that. I believe the gifted kids should have been digging further into history and working harder than their peers, because society needs citizens who can apply history's lessons to the future. I felt like the schools were failing my kids and our community.

In 5th grade, Sam's teacher "didn't do algebra," so Sam was sent to the library to work at his own pace with an algebra workbook four days a week. On the fifth day, I volunteered in his classroom to provide supplemental problem-solving challenges to a small handful of students. In contrast to my daughter's overwhelming experience, the gifted center underwhelmed my son with an education that consisted of a workbook alone in the library.

As we were growing increasingly dissatisfied with our local schools, we observed the lifestyle of our homeschooling friends. The families had freedom. They vacationed when they wanted. They spent time as a family reading and memorizing scripture. The kids could practice the piano, read books, play outside, participate in missions, community theater, cooking, or a variety of sports. And they got these things done before nightfall! How desperately we wanted our evenings back from homework and stomach aches! Family freedom was especially appealing to me as my mother was fighting cancer and I wanted the kids and me to be able to spend extended periods of time in Colorado where she lived.

Initially, my husband, Jim, was worried that I hadn't thought through what I was getting into. He asked me to present him with the first year's plan. He wanted me to establish what our educational objectives were and how we were going to meet them. My first step in coming up with that plan was to attend a HEAV (Home Educator's Association of Virginia) conference. The plethora of resources was colossal! I had no clue how to narrow down the abundance of curriculum into the right course for our family. But I asked the vendors a lot of questions, interviewed other parents, and took a stab in the dark. In the end, I used what a respected friend used since the possibilities were endless. Having finally abated Jim's worries, our homeschooling journey began. Our parents were still skeptical, but as we spent many weeks in Colorado the first year, they were able to witness our mobile school in action and became more enthusiastic.

Sam stayed home for three years, grades 6-8. We managed to keep him challenged in many subjects. He continued to play a multitude of sports and took a computer programming course online from the Stanford Education Program for Gifted Youth. His teacher didn't speak much English, and we didn't speak much C++, so that was one of his most challenging homeschooling endeavors. The kid was finally being challenged to figure something out on his own! In addition to having a lot of fun creating games with what he learned, Sam says the course sparked his interest in coding. That interest continued, and he is currently a programmer for Trip Advisor and loves what he does.

Jim, who was reluctant to pull the kids out of public school at first, became our family's biggest homeschooling fan. "I watched parents hustle their kids into their cars after baseball practice, telling them they needed to get started on homework. All I can say is that I was so glad we were done! We could just go home and play ping-pong. I also loved that my kids were 'socialized' when and where it was appropriate. People always ask me about socialization . . . I really don't think kids need to be social in the middle of science class or while learning English. The things they do need to be "socialized" in, like being a team player, negotiating, being a good friend, or giving back, can happen outside of what we think of as a traditional classroom."

One of my favorite routines was "field trip Thursdays." During our first homeschooling year, we studied American history, and we took full advantage of living in northern Virginia. Every week, we ventured somewhere for some hands-on learning. For example, as we studied Dutch immigration to America, we spent half a day at the National Gallery looking at paintings by the Dutch masters. We visited places like the National Archives, Monticello, Gettysburg, or various exhibits of the American History Museum each week. My kids felt like they were "getting out of school," and I was thrilled to take in history at our own pace and in correlation to what the kids were learning.

The family agreement was that the kids would return to public high school, and both my husband and I were ready for our son to return when the time came. He had an easy transition back into the public school. We moved to State College, Pennsylvania, after Sam's freshman year of public high school in Virginia. He attended the public school there and had a great experience! The State College Area School District bent over backwards to make sure he got an individualized education. They allowed him to take his math classes at Penn State University while still enrolled as a high schooler.

When the time came for our daughter, Jana, to go back to the public high school, she begged us to continue her education at home. At the time, we didn't know if her college options would be limited by our decision to homeschool, so we found a compromise: Northstar Academy, an accredited online Christian school. Jana was curious, self-motivated and self-disciplined. She recently told me that she hated school until she started homeschooling. She felt like much of what she did was busywork and meaningless. Homeschooling allowed her to pursue a variety of academic interests and still find time for other activities. Jana took advantage of dual-enrollment opportunities through Northstar and Bryan College, allowing her to graduate from high school a year early and from college a semester early. After taking a year off to work, she attended Fuller Theological Seminary to study marriage and family therapy and is currently completing an internship as a marriage and family therapist.

In retrospect, our entire family is grateful for our homeschooling experience. It allowed us to step back from the northern Virginia rat race that called our family to worldly things. Our kids are Christ followers, and Jim and I sometimes think their homeschooling experience during the formative adolescent years gave them the opportunity, the quiet, and the freedom to listen to God's call on their lives.

Karen Smith

Blogger; currently homeschooling (14 years)

"God, you want me to do what? You want me to homeschool my children?" I was a teacher by education, so I can only imagine what you moms who don't have an "education background" must feel when you are called to homeschool your children. I found myself bargaining with God. "Okay, God, I will homeschool them in elementary school, but they will go to school when they are in middle school and high school. I am NOT smart enough to homeschool during the high school years."

Know what I really love about God? (sarcasm inserted) He doesn't equip you for the journey ahead of time. He expects your obedience to walk in His calling, and AS you are walking in obedience, He equips you for the journey ahead.

> *May the God of peace, who through the blood of the eternal covenant brought back from the dead our Lord Jesus, that great Shepherd of the sheep, equip you with everything good for doing his will, and may he work in us what is pleasing to him, through Jesus Christ, to whom be glory forever and ever. Amen."* (Hebrews 13:20-21)

Notice the phrase "equip you with everything good for doing his will." You see, the God of peace equips us for doing His will. Hallelujah! However, when God called me to live it out—and continues to invite me to live it out—I struggled and still struggle at times with my qualifications. It doesn't matter how many times I repeat the truth; my heart still doubts. However, when doubt arrives, my job is to claim truth continually.

In May 2017, I graduated my first child from homeschool. He had been homeschooled his ENTIRE life. Never once was he enrolled in a school setting. My qualifications today are no different than they were back in 2003 when I began the homeschooling journey. I've not gone back to college and obtained another degree. However, I have learned to trust God in the calling of my life. I have learned to trust that He is at work and will equip me to give my children an excellent education. My son is now in college and is thriving. The education I was responsible for is adequate. In some ways, more than adequate.

I have two more children on the homeschool path. Each of them is uniquely different. Therefore, their education gets to be uniquely tailored to their needs. What a blessing I am allowed to give my children. There have been times I have had to release what I thought was ideal and trust God that I am walking in His calling. There have been moments when I have threatened them they were going to have to ride a school bus if they didn't get busy. There have been difficult moments. However, difficult moments do not change the calling. Difficult moments cause us to lean on Him even more! My testimony is one of God's faithfulness.

If there is one thing I have learned over the homeschool journey, it is to trust that God is in this journey. He has called, and He is equipping along the way. My sisters, if this mama can walk in His calling and graduate my children, then I am confident that you can too. Nope, we can't do it on our own, but we can do it leaning into God and allowing Him to equip us along the way.

May we not question our qualifications; rather, may we rest in His equipping.

Connie Shipe

Director of Legacy Homeschool Co-op; pastor's wife; homeschooling mom of five (11 years)

Why did you choose to homeschool? What advice can you offer to someone who is brand new to homeschooling?

The reasons to homeschool are as varied and unique as each homeschooling family. Our family chose to homeschool for many different reasons—family closeness, good Biblical curriculum, cost vs. Christian school, to name a few! The blessings of homeschooling have been even more abundant than the reasons we homeschool. Yes, we have our days of tears, but looking back over the past 11 years, I wouldn't change the precious time I have had with my kids! Some of the benefits of homeschooling for our family include the opportunity to teach my kids about God on a daily basis, the close relationship that I have with my children and they have with each other, extra time the kids get to spend with their dad on his day off, chances to do fun things as a family, vacation while most kids are in school, and more time to spend doing things the kids enjoy. I wear different hats: wife, mom, homeschool mom, pastor's wife. As a pastor's wife and a homeschool mom, I recognize that I have to have balance and keep my priorities straight. It's important to remember that you are not superwoman! God has called you first as a wife and a mom—be thankful for the season you are in. You will have opportunities for more service as your children grow older. If God has asked you to homeschool your children, He will give you the strength! Each family has a different story; ask God to show you what He has planned for you and your family at this time!

Debbie Macukas

Sixth-grade teacher; veteran homeschool parent to five children (15 years)

Much to my surprise, I did NOT ruin my sons, either academically or socially, by teaching them from elementary school through high school graduation (which, frankly, I was concerned about). One has become an accountant, and the other is graduating as a mechanical engineer in 2018—and he is accepting a job offer as I write this! More than that, they are great guys, loving men, hard workers, and they love the Lord. One of them serves as a volunteer firefighter. I say this, not to toot my own horn—believe me!!—but to say that if I, an extremely imperfect teacher and mother, can do it, anyone can. And God gets the glory! No schooling is perfect, but I would not trade those years for ANYTHING!

Some activities they were involved in were Christian Service Brigade and youth group through church (a huge part of their social and spiritual development). 4-H Club was fantastic training, as well as fun. They were stretched by doing public speaking presentations and were definitely made more community-minded. 4-H also introduced them (and me) to the fine arts, which broadened all of us. Getting to accompany my husband on business trips to Washington DC, Boston, and London (just once!) were fantastic learning opportunities (and just plain fun). We also enjoyed field trips to Colonial Williamsburg, Jamestown, Yorktown, and Gettysburg for American history and Native American studies, not to mention some wonderful African-American programs that Williamsburg had at the time. For our boys, I tried to make sure that their curiosity and individual interests were fueled and encouraged as much as possible. For our older son, it was photography and videography, art museums, and music. For our youngest, it was all of the hands-on, science-y things we could find without burning down the house or exploding things! I also purposely hooked him up with godly men who could put him to work and teach him skills like carpentry. I think the first thing he did was to "help" with a redo of a preschool building by pulling nails out of old flooring.

As for curriculum, I loved Sonlight when they were young. The read-alouds were their favorites. I used Teaching Textbooks math in grades 6-8, and we all loved it. Geometry in that series was a disappointment; eventually, I used Math-U-See for that. For writing, I had fairly good success with "Institute for Excellence in Writing" materials. (Mr. Pudewa's videos did have a tendency to make us doze off, however.) The boys have both said that they went back to some of his teachings during college writing assignments. The spelling program that he advocates was the turning point in finally teaching our youngest to spell—in ninth grade!! Science was Apologia, hands-down! For chemistry, we had a group of thirteen kids come to our house once a month to do the labs. I facilitated, and they did it in teams. They had a blast. I knew nothing about chemistry, but they helped each other. Afterwards, the girls stayed inside and wrote nice, neat lab reports and chatted with me. The boys scribbled down their reports and went outside to play with air rifles! For health, history, and government, I ended up going back to Abeka. It was just clearer, easier, and made life livable!

God bless you!

Leigh Anne Rufener

Pastor's wife; women's ministry leader; former public school math teacher; homeschool mom of three (9 years)

Why did you choose to homeschool?

When our son was preschool age, we began to think about schooling options. My husband and I had differing opinions on preschool, mostly due to our own personal experiences. This was the beginning of our seeking out of educational options for our children.

As we began embarking upon this journey, we began to realize that, in order for us to aid our children in seeing the world through the lens of Christ, the gospel, and faith, we knew that homeschooling would be the best option. Also, since my husband and I were once public school educators, we realized that our children would get the most one-on-one assistance through homeschooling. Due to my husband's ministry job, and wanting to prioritize our family time, we had to think outside the box. Homeschooling gave us the flexibility and freedom to be together regularly, to take as many field trips as we thought necessary, and the option to travel and visit family and friends as needed.

What is your method? Describe it.

I am a Starbucks Mama. I VASTLY value community and culture, yet I am passionate about a solid, Jesus-centered academic education. The best way to describe our homeschool is traditionally & classically eclectic. We are part of a wonderful Classical Conversations community with a child in Foundations, Essentials, and the Challenge A program. The classical model, combined with our faith, gives me a solid foundation. It is incredibly important for a homeschool parent to also school in a way that brings him or her life, so I also add my own flair to the process! That is why I begin this section with "I am a Starbucks Mama," because schooling at coffee shops & bookstores is a favorite of mine (and my boys!).

How have you schooled through difficult circumstances?

Our family has had to overcome many challenging life situations. The key has been to continually give thanks in all circumstances. Simply stated: life can be hard, but we are blessed. Throughout our homeschooling journey, we have planted a church and walked through numerous ministry challenges and blessings. Recently, our family completely transitioned from one denomination to another. Our family has had many health struggles. My husband has had three surgeries—one being a 6-month recovery with the surgery being at a world-renowned hospital three hours away. There have been various hospital visits and stays. In 2016, one of our sons received multiple concussions from various falls/accidents that have led to long-term repercussions, which we continue to address through doctor appointments (many hours away) and therapies. There have been various extended family trials and emotional challenges, primarily due to grieving the loss of several close family members. For many years, I led a women's ministry in our community. And . . . I ran a business through it all. Please hear my heart. I do not share all of this for notoriety or to be seen as a saint. I share this because the Lord has been a constant source of strength, grace, hope, joy, and grace through it all. I have seen firsthand the work that the Lord can do in a heart that is hard and aching. God gives strength for the weary, hope for the hopeless, and grace for the journey. I have been reminded to do the next BEST thing in love, and do ALL things for God's ultimate glory. Truly, life is all about knowing God and making Him known. And this begins with our family!

How has homeschooling changed you as a person?

How hasn't homeschooling changed me as a person? Homeschooling our three boys has changed my life! This journey has taught me more than I could have ever thought. God does not always call us to do what is easy, but what is best. With that being said, I have often went back to our "why" when it gets tough, which it will. I do not say that to be negative, but to be real. The Bible says that "in this life we will have trials, but take heart, I have overcome the world." (John 16:33)

I have learned in a tangible way that I am in desperate need of the grace and strength of God, every moment of every day!

I have realized yet again the depths of my sin. At times, I feel that homeschooling pulls all of the yuck out of me. Perseverance and persistence are the key to continuing in this journey. I am so grateful for these times of growth. They have made me even more passionate about education and have helped me become more flexible and gracious. What a redeeming God we serve!

I am learning that everyone learns at a different pace AND that every child has differing strengths and weaknesses. I must remember this and where I came from, and never forget that our boys desperately need Jesus, the gospel, and faith ALL the time—JUST LIKE ME!

Above all, homeschooling has made me a person who advocates for her boys, is passionate about raising boys, and honored & thankful beyond words to have this opportunity to school these amazing boys every day, by God's amazing grace!

Eva Tomashefski

MS in education; homeschooled her daughter (7 1/2 years)

My adopted daughter and I have had quite an educational journey. I would like to share our story with you. It is my hope that you'll be encouraged to boldly step forward, advocate for your children, and recognize the many opportunities and alternatives available.

We brought our daughter home from an orphanage in Poland when she was 2 1/2 years old. We enrolled her two hoursa day, two days a week in preschool within a few months of her arrival. I attended preschool with her for the first month in order to help with any language barriers and observe her behavior with the other children. At that time, the teacher indicated it was a good move since she had some social issues that needed attention. In first grade, I began to notice an inconsistency with her work. Papers from the school were also not making it home and we missed many communications from the school. It was a chaotic year, and my daughter said, "My teacher lost her smile."

I requested a meeting early in her 2nd grade year to discuss my concerns. No one seemed to be concerned. As the year progressed I was having a great deal of difficulty getting her out the door to her bus on time. The work that was coming from school was of much poorer quality than the work done at home. My frustration was increasing, and so was hers. In March of that school year, I received a report card with seven areas marked as "needing attention." I had not received one contact prior to this, indicating that there was a problem. I contacted the school counselor by phone to discuss my concerns and she started to put me off saying that some children just mature later than others. I interrupted her and said—we are talking about seven areas marked as "needing attention," not seven areas marked as "making progress." I emailed the school principal with a written request for a psychological evaluation and made arrangements to volunteer in the classroom. I noticed my daughter was very distracted and although she remained in her seat, she was always fiddling with something. I could see that much of the time she and several others were not hearing and understanding all of the directions given.

My request for an evaluation with the school psychologist was granted in the beginning of her 3rd grade year. The psychologist's first comment was, "We are not tapping into what this child is capable of." She validated all of my concerns and then some. Behavioral checklists indicated Attention Deficit Disorder, Inattentive type, which was confirmed by her medical doctor.

Testing indicated my daughter also had a learning disability in reading. It was another month before any special education services began twice a week, but her needs were still not being addressed adequately. My daughter's self-esteem was plummeting and she was giving up on academics. I had positive relationships with school personnel in the past. My son had gone through this school three years previously with high academic standing. In addition, I had served on the PTA and coordinated the book fairs. When I began to advocate for my daughter, those relationships became strained, and I did not expect the resistance I encountered. The guidance counselor said my daughter was at the bottom of the social spectrum and suggested it was due to her one blind eye and we should do something about it. When talking about the ADD, she said the reason for this behavior was due to a lack of structure in the home. I found her comments to be insensitive and judgmental. Having been a school psychologist previously, I was disappointed to see how a parent could be treated so insensitively.

Children struggling with learning disabilities often require a much different parenting style than children who do not struggle with these issues. The parenting techniques used to raise my three older children were not as effective with my daughter and it took some time to realize what adaptations needed to be made. She required a much higher degree of accountability for a longer period of time than my other children. Following through took extra commitment and energy. Many parents of children with learning disabilities face challenges beyond typical child-rearing, and it is important for educators and others to be sensitive to this.

I began to explore other educational opportunities. I was intimidated about the idea of homeschooling until some homeschool moms invited me to their homes and I saw how feasible it was. I met with the school principal in February and said that I was considering homeschooling. She encouraged me to try it, saying she had seen some remarkable things with homeschoolers. She recommended trying it for the remainder of that school year, and if it didn't work out we could re-enroll her at the beginning of her 4th grade year. So that March, I began homeschooling. My first goal was to awaken my daughter to a love of learning and build up her self-esteem. I found a checklist of positive attributes in the *ADHD Book of Lists* by Sandra Reif and taped it to our refrigerator. Whenever she would get frustrated and say that she was stupid, I would march her over to the fridge and we'd go down the list of all the beautiful attributes she had. Although we had some difficult moments, I always tried to communicate to her that we are a team and we are going to get through this! One of the books we read was *A Door in the Wall.* I highly recommend it for anyone who struggles with a handicap, learning disability, or feelings of inadequacy. It is a wonderful story about a boy who becomes crippled after having polio. A monk takes him in and helps him to find his door in the wall—the thing that he can do well.

I must admit that in the beginning I was overwhelmed with all the information at my disposal to teach her. After lamenting to one of my homeschool friends who had been a certified English teacher, she said to me "Just have her read, read, read, and write, write, write." That was the best advice I could have ever received. I began to formulate a philosophy of education on my own and I realized it was all about input and output: helping your child learn to take in information, process it by using it to better themselves or problem-solve, and then express it in a form that others could understand.

My daughter despised reading as it was a frustrating process for her, so we started with short reading passages from a daily devotional. She found the *My America* and *Dear America* books appealing because they were diaries written by young girls like herself, and they tied in nicely with history. Writing had been a source of frustration for her, but one time when I told her to sit and write anything that came to mind I was amazed at how she took off! She wrote pages and pages. Her creativity just poured out of her. From that point on, all her spelling, grammar, and conventions were taught by editing these creative drafts. At the end of the semester she had a beautifully finished story—she even illustrated it.

As a homeschooler, I was not under the same time constraints that the teachers were to get through a particular curriculum within a certain period of time. Therefore, we were able to emphasize my daughter's reading, writing, and math skills until we were certain that she had learned them adequately. Once she was given the opportunity to work at her own pace in a distraction free environment, and she knew that I would not accept work that was of poor quality (we didn't have to move on to something else until she had done it right!), she began to blossom. I saw her self-esteem improve as she saw that she could do these things and gained confidence in herself.

It was working. People started to comment on how much calmer and more confident my daughter seemed to be. We also started to become aware of her artistic talent. She was blossoming as an artist and musician. She would spend hours of her time drawing and playing her violin. TV time was strictly monitored and limited in our home, and I strongly believe this was a huge factor in what allowed these other talents to emerge. One of the biggest myths about homeschooling is that the children are "socially deprived." Because we were doing 1:1 instruction, we were able to finish our school day earlier than public school children, and my daughter never had homework. She was free during the after-school time to play with friends and do other activities that she would not have been able to do at public school because it took her so long to complete work. She had lots of sleepovers on the weekends and maintained a very active social life through Girl Scouts, homeschool groups, and church groups. I homeschooled her full-time for two and a half years (second half of 3rd grade through 5th), then we homeschooled part-time (English, Health, PE, and social studies) for 6th through 11th grade while she took art, orchestra, math, and science classes in public school. She attended public school full-time her 12th grade year and graduated with her friends.

For her, doing the public school/home school combination was the best of both worlds. I am grateful that my daughter and I had this time together. We have a good relationship, and we laugh together. She excelled in her art, took formal art classes in Italy while in college, and is now an illustrator.

Mary Sellers

Lecturer in English, Pennsylvania State University; PhD candidate in American studies; veteran homeschool mom to four children (18 years)

Over the course of eighteen years of homeschooling five children, I learned a number of things, mostly through trial and error. I would like to share two important lessons with you. Both items deal with things central to the homeschool life—curriculum and schedule. Yet I found that the same principle helped me to determine both of them.

Like most of you, I pored over curriculum catalogs and eagerly awaited the curriculum fair. All the different programs seemed so wonderful, and I was always sure if I found just the right one, I'd become that organized, amazing homeschool mom that I had pictured in my mind, and my children would adore spelling and math and writing. What I found was, if the curriculum didn't fit me as a teacher, there was no way I could adapt it to fit my family. I am not a person who thrives on writing everything down or on intensive lesson planning. I know I love to read. I know I like things to be as simple as possible. I know I hate textbooks. Guess what? The year I thought the workbook and textbook-based curriculum would be a great idea was a colossal failure.

Was it the curriculum? No, it was that I, as a teacher, did not thrive under that system. I changed to a read-aloud, literature- and writing-centered curriculum. My enthusiasm for what I chose carried over to my children, and because I loved the way I was teaching them, I was able to get through the whiny days. Choose what suits your teaching style. You can try the complex curriculum which promises to turn your family into the most organized, efficient homeschoolers in the co-op, but if you are bored and stressed, your children will be too.

Along the same lines, I wanted an organized and efficient schedule, and I was able to achieve that despite all the planning books I read which recommended checklists and plans to get the day started early. But the reality was that we liked to sleep in. No one in the family voluntarily got out of bed before 7:00, including mom. As the keeper of my home, I had to take into account how we functioned best, especially in the years with nursing babies and toddlers. What worked for me was less of a schedule and more of "anchor points." School started after breakfast, and the first item was always math. It did not matter if school began at 8:30 or 10:00—math was first. That way, if one child dawdled or I had to deal with little ones, no one wondered what happened first. The second anchor point was at 11:00; everything stopped for our read-aloud time. This is where we would have religious instruction, reading history or literature, and general discussion of things for the day.

What can you take away from my mistakes and successes? I hope that you will realize that you as a parent and teacher know your family better than anyone else. Just because a schedule or a curriculum worked for someone else does not mean it will work for you and for this stage of your lives. There is no right way to do things, no magical curriculum which will solve all of your problems. Homeschooling is both joy and misery, but mostly it is the everyday—checking the math, giving spelling tests, making sure they understand photosynthesis and the causes for the Civil War, ensuring they emptied the dishwasher and brushed their teeth. Take a good look at what makes you excited as a teacher and what makes your children excited. Assess the flow of your day. Sometimes just a little change here and there is all it takes to go from the life you have to the life you wish you had.

Nancy McTernan

Veteran homeschool mom to three children (4 years)

I was excited to hear about homeschooling before I even had children of my own (before 1976). My interest in it stems from my own dislike of early schooling. I realize not every child disliked school but I sure did. Homeschooling could tailor the teaching to match the child's interests, talents and personality. A parent who raises a child for their first six years of life could continue to teach them. This sounded good to me.

Years later, three of our children were in public school. There were some excellent teachers, but I found it hard to get involved with their schooling beyond some homework assignments. When God was taken out of the public schools, we enrolled our children in a Christian school. (Proverbs 22:6)

At this time (1990), our daughter was to have surgery and would possibly miss a lot of school. My interest in homeschooling returned as an option. I felt unqualified but read many books on the subject. I was ready to give it a try. We gave our oldest two children the choice to stay in public school or homeschool. My daughter decided to stay out of the adventure, but my sons jumped in, so what was set in motion became a reality.

It was exciting times for homeschooling. There were only a few established curriculums. Our book fairs were held in local church basements. Many parents presented and packaged their own curriculums. Creativity was exploding. Today book fairs are held in huge auditoriums.

Ask any homeschool mom or dad how their teaching connects with life events. (Deuteronomy 6:7) God inspires insight, and connections just happen. A subject like crystals can lead to Louis Pasteur. From Pasteur you can connect to rabies, to bacteria, to wine fermentation, etc.

It is such a blessing to not just read a report card but to experience your child's creativity. Another blessing is the whole family involvement in the learning process. There are history and science fairs as well as field trips, lots of field trips!

Homeschooling is not for everyone. It is time-consuming, especially with multiple children on different age levels. A good program, however, can compensate for your weakness. I used Saxon math, a solid program, to overcome my weakness in math. My original goal was to tailor teaching to the child's interest and personality.

Nikki McTernan, M.Ed.

Certified K-6 teacher; currently homeschooling her three girls (7 years)

I have a certificate in elementary education and have passed the exams and completed the coursework, field studies, and teaching practicum associated with that license. The mentor teacher and 1st grade students from my teaching practicum will always hold a fond place in my heart. I have also worked as a substitute teacher in public schools and as a cyber school teacher. In doing all of this, I have met an assortment of wonderful educators and advisers, as well as fascinating children. In becoming a homeschooling mom, I found my own children to be the most endearing and delightful pupils of all. The experiences associated with obtaining and upholding the teaching license greatly contributed to the comfort level and confidence I felt in transitioning to teaching my own children at home.

As I complete the necessary continuing education hours involved in keeping my certificate active, our homeschooling endeavors and my own mental and overall well-being benefit. Learning with kids is wonderfully satisfying and exciting, and so is the lifelong pursuit of adult learning and improvement. Just last week, we watched a butterfly emerge from a pupa and used some resources received as part of a continuing education seminar to extend our learning and to create nature journal entries. The continuing education hours are a welcome requirement, and any homeschooling parent can engage in continuing his or her own education by making it a point to utilize the often free and stimulating podcasts available. There are also homeschooling conventions and seminars, thought-provoking books, and gatherings of like-minded parents readily available.

The vast quantity of time homeschooling families spend together provides countless chances to build sibling relationships, and even to involve grandparents and spouses in the learning adventures. To share so many connections and points of reference is a deep blessing. Attitude plays an important role as well. For example, while there are always logistics involved in incorporating new family members, the main thrust can be ushering in an attitude of babies being a blessing and not a burden to the homeschooling experience. Perspective is key, and everything gets completed in due time. Classroom teaching and homeschool teaching are both guaranteed to keep life interesting, as no two days are the same. It is also important to note that, while home is the wonderful center of the homeschool experience, there are also plenty of valuable homeschooling experiences found outside of the home.

Classroom teachers often post or create classroom rules or mission statements. Moms can also create mission statements for their own children. I run my decisions through a filter mission of giving our children an abundant and unrushed childhood, where they grow up learning to crave and love that which is good and true and lovely. My husband and I feel that homeschooling provides the best opportunity for us to provide this type of atmosphere. We also feel that homeschooling is as much a lifestyle choice as an educational choice. While I do not at all think that homeschooling parents need to hold a teaching certificate to teach well, I am grateful for the seamless way mine has meshed with the homeschooling mom I am today. Blessings to all of you on your homeschooling journey!

Rebecca John

Homeschooled; BS in engineering; currently homeschooling five children (8 years)

Homeschooling has been definitive in my life in many ways. Growing up, I saw my parents stop, consider, and make different choices about things many people see as automatic, such sending your kids to school! It helped me see that it's important to think about and live by your beliefs and convictions, and not just go along with the flow in life. My parents began homeschooling in Pennsylvania in the 1980s, and there was no homeschool law, which meant that every school district decided what they thought was legal for homeschoolers. I remember going with my parents to the capital to lobby our state representatives to pass a bill to make homeschooling legal—talk about an education in civics!

For us, homeschooling created a very tight-knit family, and I have many amazing memories of things we learned and experiences we had together. Family trips were often field trips to important historical sites, and dinner conversation usually involved current events, history lessons, science or math concepts, or speaking with guests from many places around the world. Of course, we had to learn some things that didn't seem interesting at the time, but often, learning was diving into a concept with all our senses, like reading books about Native Americans, then creating a longhouse in our basement, weaving wampum, and eating succotash for dinner that night.

As I grew older, my parents encouraged me to gradually become more independent in my learning, as well as learn from a variety of different sources (textbooks, video courses, homeschool classes, labs, college courses, etc.). By the time I went to college to get my engineering degree, I felt prepared to take the ownership of my own learning that a university degree requires. Now that I am an adult, I feel like homeschooling has given me two things: a love of learning (my favorite activity is still to curl up with a good book), and the grounding and confidence to forge my own path in line with my personal values in life. Looking back, I can see the ways my parents challenged me to think outside the norm, and I value the confidence it's given me as an adult.

I LOVED being homeschooled, especially after attending college classes and realizing how much I love individualized education where I can learn at my own pace. Each educational system has its strengths and weaknesses, but in a classroom, there is simply no way to meet each individual's own needs and pacing. The class must move together, and so there will be times when the student either feels lost because he requires more explanation, or he has to sit through yet another review of material he has already mastered. The strength of homeschooling is that each child can be known and guided along the path of becoming a life-long learner at their own pace and in the way that meets their own individual needs.

Because of my personal experience, I always wanted to homeschool my own kids. When they were little we read LOTS of books, played games to help them learn about life, and spent a lot of time outdoors, so homeschooling was a natural extension of those early years. A classroom setting for very young children, especially in today's current educational climate, seemed developmentally inappropriate for my little ones who loved to be read to and learn through play. Also, because of some learning and sensory issues, I felt like homeschooling would allow my children to learn and flourish at their own pace, without the added burden of feeling out-of-sync with their peers. Plus, it gave us the freedom to tailor learning in a way that helped each child succeed.

Even though I was homeschooled, I felt like being the homeschooling parent was an entirely new experience! Every new job has a learning curve, and I think the same is true as a homeschooling parent. You will never pick the perfect curriculum, have the perfect lesson plan, the perfect schedule, the right balance of extracurricular activities, etc. So for me, I initially felt as though I had to get it right the first time, and often worried that I was failing my kids. I also put a lot of pressure on myself and my kids to do things a certain way, follow the curriculum just so, and learn according to a certain schedule. I ended up stressed out, worried, and unhappy, and my kids certainly didn't enjoy it either! Learning flexibility and following my children's individual learning timelines made such a difference! Children learn to read when they are ready, and trying to rush the process or worry over them being behind is counterproductive. Children are natural learners, so freeing them up to do that allows the parents to guide them in the natural learning process. In fact, parents are uniquely positioned to be the best teacher for their own child because they know the child best and can tailor learning to fit the individual child according to their needs.

The biggest piece of advice I have for new homeschooling parents is to READ to their kids. Read as much and as often as you can to your kids. Encourage them to read for fun. And don't stop reading to them when they learn to read. Reading to your kids is one of the biggest factors in their academic success. I would also encourage parents that there will be times when they wonder if they are doing enough. Being able to spend quality time with your children, and having input into not just their academic learning, but the formation of their character is priceless. And don't worry that you don't know enough to teach them; just learn right along with them. In fact, seeing you learn might be the best education they can get.

I have five children now, ages 3 months to 10 years, and homeschooling can be a juggling act! I try to combine all the subjects I can and just customize it for each age. So we do a lot of reading together, and most of our history, science, art, physical education, field trips, etc. are together. Math and language arts are individual, so I give each child individual help in these areas when the little ones are napping or playing with their other siblings. Nap time is a great time to get the more "intensive" subjects taken care of with older kids. I also try to give my little ones individual attention early in the day by reading to them and playing games with them. Then they are content to play on their own for a while, or do "school" (coloring, etc.) with the older ones. My younger children learn SO much by just being around my older kids. For hundreds of years, one-room schoolhouses had all ages learning together and the older ones helped the younger ones. That concept works well with homeschooling families too! Also, finding a community of homeschoolers to ask questions and trade ideas with has been so helpful. Parents need encouragement, and kids need to make friends!

I felt like being homeschooled was a valuable gift my parents gave me, and I am excited to give it to my children.

Abigail Bourne

Director of Class Act Productions; writer; actress; was homeschooled for 13 years

"So, what's it like to have been homeschooled? Did you like it?" Any student who has gone through this "unorthodox" process of education has heard these oft-repeated questions. Home-schooling, interestingly enough, is becoming a more accessible and acceptable educational style in this culture, primarily due to this method's ability to conform to the individual needs of a student.

However, as I think back over my experience of growing up in the homeschool world, the idea of individual styles of learning was not my parents' focus. Don't get me wrong, my parents certainly were aware of my educational strengths and weaknesses, but their goal was not merely that shortsighted. Homeschooling was so much beyond education; it was an opportunity—the call, if you will, to raise up a generation of individuals who were discipled in the ways of the Lord and desired to serve and follow Him above all else. Perhaps that sounds lofty, but I firmly believe that that vision was what enabled my parents to continue without wavering through all the hardships and challenges homeschool families face.

As I write this, I know this thought of having a greater driving principle can seem overwhelming to an idea that is already frighteningly huge. Yet, it is what allowed so much more freedom in our home. My mom wasn't constantly consumed by the impracticality of tailoring each lesson to the student. ("Life is busy" is the understatement of the year to a homeschool mom.) It gave a purpose greater than individual achievement, and it cultivated a ministry mindset.

Granted, each homeschool family enters into this venture for various reasons and with varying philosophies. Education is right, good, necessary, and something to be sought after with excellence, and when coupled with a vision that goes beyond the immediate, it has the potential to grow individuals able impact the world to which they are called.

Were there struggles? Yes! Was there laughter? Yes! Was I a problem student? Oh, yeah! Still, through the exciting learning moments, the tears, the joy, I have experienced life. There is nothing sheltered about homeschooling! Plus, any trip could be turned into a "great learning experience" (homeschool mom strikes again!)

My mom has now finished her final year of homeschooling. By May of 2018, she completed 33 years of schooling, teaching eleven children from pre-K through 12th grade! She is truly a remarkable woman. Her faithfulness to her purpose and her desire to honor the Lord in this call is such a wonderful example. But she would be the first to say that it is not because *she* is so extraordinary or amazing that she has been successful in this call, but rather because we serve a faithful God whose mercies are new every morning.

Did I like being homeschooled? I never knew anything else—but yes, I did. Would I ever consider homeschooling? Of course; I mean, my mom made it look so easy. Is it worth it? I guess that depends on your goal. I have had the extraordinary blessing of not only being homeschooled but also homeschooling for a time. Both have enriched my life greatly, both were undertaken with the desire to educate and the vision to disciple and that makes a difference.

So, what would I say to encourage a family just beginning this homeschooling adventure? Make it easy on yourself, don't stress about having the perfect curriculum that will make your student a future Nobel prize winner. Instead, have a vision and don't give up—ever! If your goal is to build the kingdom of God and work for His glory through homeschooling your children, you cannot possibly fail.

Jeff and Ruthi Martin

Organizers of the State College Homeschool Book Sale (Pennsylvania);
veteran homeschool parents to four children (20 years)

What made you decide to homeschool?

We initially stepped into homeschooling based on a positive impression Jeff had in college. He befriended a Christian family that homeschooled, and he grew to admire them. He became convinced that homeschooling was a wise choice. Ruthi was hesitant at first, so as a compromise Jeff did the first year of homeschool with our oldest, teaching her to read using Benjamin Blumenfeld's book *How to Tutor*. (This no-nonsense book provides well-planned lessons for reading, writing, and arithmetic).

Our primary motive for homeschooling was to provide a Christian education and curriculum. Ruthi and I met at a Christian summer camp and encouraged each other to raise our own family with the same spirit of Christian values and fun that we enjoyed at the summer camp. We also wanted to challenge ourselves personally to be willing to grow and learn as needed to educate and disciple our children.

Were there any roadblocks in the beginning you had to overcome? If so, how?

The initial roadblock was Ruthi's reservation about homeschooling. Her own prior experience with homeschooling was not very positive. The few homeschool families that she knew on the surface seemed strange and awkward, and her own parents and siblings, while not disparaging, were also hesitant about the idea. So our initial compromise was to try homeschooling out for size with simply skipping kindergarten and teaching our oldest to read. The Pennsylvania homeschool law also facilitated this decision, because parents are not legally obligated to send their children to school or even register as a homeschool family until children are age 8 (though Philadelphia's compulsory age is 6).

Our feeling is that if Christians are uncertain about homeschooling, it may still be in the child's best interest to simply skip kindergarten, 1st, and 2nd grades with a stay-at-home parent who reads the Bible and good books to their children. That alone will accomplish much in sowing the seeds of good Christian morals and understanding. This point is made well in *Better Late Than Early: A New Approach to Your Child's Education* by Dorothy N. Moore and Raymond Moore.

What curriculum did you choose?

We did not choose a single curriculum provider, but we used the publishers that we felt were best in each subject and also worked well for each of our students. For example, we used *Saxon Math* for all of our children, but took a detour with some of them and later used *Jacobs Geometry*. For English we used *Abeka* for grammar, *Jensens* for high school essay writing, *Writing Strands* for creative writing, and *Vocabulary Cartoons* for high school vocabulary. Our favorite science curriculum was *Apologia*, and history was *Story of the World* and later *Omnibus*.

During the elementary years it was just lots of reading, 3-5 hours a day, wagon loads of library books, taking advantage of our library's *Young Authors* contests every year, drawing and writing, field trips, etc.

What is the greatest benefit you've found from doing it?

Each of our children has been given a foundation in basic educational needs to prepare them for their future, along with the privilege and blessing of learning about God from the Bible with a thorough explanation of the good news. There are so many lies about God and the Christian faith being promoted in America and world culture today that decisive action must be taken to counter these lies. Homeschooling provides an opportunity to sow good seeds into the lives of our children while the "cement is still wet."

Of course, even if you homeschool, there is no guarantee that your children will choose to follow Christ. We knew this objectively and now also personally, because not all of our children have chosen to follow Christ after our best efforts at Christian homeschooling.

Homeschooling is good and useful, and we would homeschool again in a heartbeat. However, we appreciate that Christian homeschooling can never make someone a Christian, but only the power of God's spirit.

Any advice you'd give a new homeschooling parent?

If you live in Pennsylvania, children under age 8 are not required to attend school. Take advantage of this law to test drive homeschooling if you have doubts as we did. Both parents need to be committed to the effort. Be prepared to challenge yourself to grow personally into the role of a Christian homeschool parent. It will require an investment of your time and money to read good books, join homeschool support groups, and attend Christian homeschool conferences.

Finally, one of our children completed their freshman year of college during their senior year of homeschool, killing two birds with one stone. Our children took advantage of free room and board at home, helping them to earn college degrees without any debt, which is a great blessing.

We will pray for you that you will seek God and fulfill the calling of Christian parenting, one of the greatest works of a lifetime.

Elizabeth Hagerup

Missionary with Disciplemakers; currently homeschooling seven children (12 years)

Can you share how homeschool has helped your child with autism?

When my fifth son was diagnosed with "mild to moderate autism spectrum disorder," I had already been homeschooling his elder siblings for several years. The experts strongly discouraged us from homeschooling him, and we tried an autism preschool for one semester. The teachers were kind, but he clearly wanted to be at home. In our case, homeschooling has been a wonderful fit. Since one of the primary needs of a child with autism is help with social skills, at home he gets continual training by interacting with his siblings in a safe, loving environment. Academically, I have been able to use the same curriculum I use with his siblings (through 4th grade) though he does need more help and repetition.

Patrice

BA in psychology; single mom; currently homeschooling her son (2 years)

About three years ago, when my son was in third grade, I felt what I believed to be an urging from the Holy Spirit to homeschool. Prior to this revelation, I considered the idea off and on, but didn't think that I could handle such a task being a single mother, working full-time, and finishing research at Penn State University. Also, my son loved school. He was very social and intelligent, having been placed in the highest level of academics for his grade level, excelled in Spanish and Chinese, and had been classically trained in piano since age three. This child was brilliant. But what God showed me was that he was lacking the most important thing: *the fruits of the Holy Spirit!*

God does not measure success the way humans do; we are limited to this realm. God-like success involves the character and spirit of man. I realized that if I did not heed the Lord's calling, I would be quenching God's purpose for his life. The seeds of one's character, both good and bad, are planted as a child, and they continue to grow and produce deep roots. I want my son's deep roots to be planted in the Lord, which produces love, joy, peace, patience, kindness, goodness, faithfulness, gentleness, and self-control.

Although it was hard, I chose to be obedient to the clear leading I had from the Lord, and I pulled him out of school. If God truly

193

instructed me to homeschool and disciple my son, then He would give me a strategic plan and supernatural strength. I employed all of my support systems and we started homeschooling with Pennsylvania Cyber. I incorporated additional materials to ensure that his spiritual needs were met.

In the morning, we would each read our devotions (his was a Veggietales devotional and mine was Our Daily Bread online). We would discuss what the Lord was showing us, pray for the day, and intercede for others. Afterwards, he would eat breakfast, start cyber school and I would be off to work.

I began to see a wonderful change in his spirit and desire for more of God. He chose on his own to be baptized and attend a Bible study. His heart was truly changing, and I was grateful to God for the visible transformation.

There are times of struggle, and that's when God's strength is made perfect. Like when I have to send my son to another state to visit his father, or when I doubt I can handle the task of homeschooling. He is the one who gives us the ability to fight against defeat, discouragement, and lies from the enemy. During these times I also reach out to my saved girlfriends for fellowship and prayer to regain strength.

I know that choosing to be obedient to God and homeschool my son was the best decision. What an honor it is to be able to shape your child's character and debunk the myths of the carnal world. We are their teachers and light-bearers in a time where there is so much darkness and evil. We are raising an army of God-fearing children who will stand up to bullies and stand for Christ. "Train a child in the way that he should go and when he is old he will not depart from it." (Proverbs 22:6)

Terri Verlinde

Real estate agent; veteran homeschool parent to four children (5 years)

My husband is from South Africa and was raised in the tradition of the Dutch Reformed Church. In South Africa and The Netherlands at that time, public schooling for children was largely "Christian" and often associated with the church. In many cases, particular congregations gave a part of their tithes and offerings to support the Christian education of their own families' children. When we were married and had children of our own, Hans was completely unfamiliar with the American education system, and we were both completely unfamiliar with the idea of homeschooling. We took a great leap of faith and decided to approach the education of our children in what we thought was a very unconventional way, with their best interests in mind.

When our oldest was approaching school age, we had a number of local friends who were homeschooling at the time, and we all shared a common concern about the impact of humanism and the godless socialization of our children in the public school. With these concerns, a small group of us decided to begin a day-school/homeschool co-op that we believe addressed the needs of our children. Eventually, this day-school became unsustainable due to the advanced educational needs of the high school children, and the school folded. The homeschool co-op branch of this school continued to serve many local families and has impact to this day.

When our day-school folded, a number of the families enrolled in a private school which also folded in time. Our family then explored the option of cyber-schooling, and eventually our oldest child graduated from this cyber school. During her high school years, she was able to take some college courses and achieved the status of National Merit Scholar. This allowed her to receive a full scholarship to a private Christian college. We are thankful for the opportunities that she had with the flexibility of the cyber-school. She married another student at the college, and we are all now blessed with their first child!

The experience of our oldest child set the stage for the schooling of our next three children, and each benefitted greatly from the variety of schooling options. Though not always "homeschooled," they have benefitted from "parent-directed" education in each situation. Each of our children has different needs, and though it can be a challenge to recognize these needs, every parent knows their child better than anyone else and is equipped to decide how to best educate their children.

It has been a blessing for our children to find and maintain friendships within our local homeschooling community and to work and learn with other families who are striving toward similar goals and facing similar challenges in our daily lives.

Nadia

Dental hygienist; single mom homeschooling her daughter (5 years)

Why did you decide to homeschool?

I saw that my daughter was displaying bad behavior after starting kindergarten, and the behavior got worse with each passing year. I realized she was being influenced way too much by her peers in a negative way. This concerned me, and I brought this concern to the Lord. Soon after, a homeschool mom gave me a documentary to watch about public schools and what they are required to teach the kids. Some of it went against the biblical truths I valued and my heart was even more troubled.

Homeschooling was never something that even entered my mind because I was a single parent and thought I wouldn't be able to do it. However, after asking other homeschoolers questions, I realized it was possible for me to include it into our lives. I had my small group pray for me to be able hear God's voice in what He desires for me to do. The next day, God impressed it upon my heart how important it was for me to disciple my daughter. I realized this was a once-in-a-lifetime opportunity that will produce a harvest of benefits. I knew it was going to be a challenging endeavor, but I was convinced the Lord wanted me to enter into this new journey and trusted Him to be my strength and provider.

Deuteronomy 6:7 says to teach my child all throughout the day about God. This was impossible to do while she was away in school for most of the day. As I responded in obedience, the Lord has been faithful in leading me and guiding me. We do devotionals daily which often turns into fruitful discussions that sometimes last for an hour! I love having the opportunity not to rush to school, but to start off our day by inviting the Lord into our lives. Through God's word and discipleship, my daughter has had a heart change and has fallen in love with Jesus. She is now the influencer . . . trying to be the light in this world and telling others about the Lord. She has developed so many wonderful characteristics that reflect Jesus's. I am thankful for how God has used this homeschooling journey to bring so much joy and love into our lives. I am excited to see how He will continue to do His work in us (I say "us," because God did a lot of changing in me as well.)

How do you balance work, home life, and teaching?

I feel fortunate that I only work part-time, which makes it possible for me to teach her. Each year is a bit different but, for the most part, we follow a similar schedule. When my daughter was younger, I went over her lessons the evening before my workday to make sure she understood what to do. She did her school work in the morning while I was at work, and later in the day I would correct it. If my daughter completed all that was required of her, she would be allowed to go to her swim practice or other fun activities in the evening. Staying on task is very important in staying sane. I believe you must constantly practice self-control and discipline to homeschool while being a working single parent. I'm far from perfect at this, but I always strive to be consistently disciplined in this.

Do you have any advice for a single parent that wants to homeschool?

Make sure it is a calling from God. Try to only work part-time and have a strong support group. God connected us with many other homeschoolers who were often willing to take my daughter to a field trip with them or have her over for a day while I worked. We also participated in co-ops 1-2 times a week. These things always motivate kids and give them a sense of joy and excitement and help them develop friendships.

Also, I know it's easy to just be laid back with your plans and stretch out your days and do whatever you feel like doing, but . . . I would strongly encourage you to have a routine and, as the kids get older, have them get up at a certain time and take more responsibility over their work and time management. I've seen some kids get lazy through homeschooling. Now that my daughter is 13, I've challenged her to set her own alarm clock and to get up on her own. I help her learn how to manage her time and how to complete certain assignments on her own by the end of the week. My advice is to keep challenging your child each year. Chat with other homeschoolers for ideas and support.

As a homeschool mom, be prepared to have off days. Accept every hardship as an opportunity to teach and disciple your kids. So when you face a challenge, when they are not listening, when things are not going your way, stop and seize the moment to give God glory through discipleship.

I would not recommend leaving your child home alone while working full-time or even 3-4 days per week. The Enemy loves to tempt us when we are all alone and no one can see us. My daughter gave into some temptations because she was on her own a lot; for a few months, I was gone about 4-5 days a week. If you work a lot throughout the week and still desire to homeschool, I would suggest making arrangements for the child/children to be supervised by an adult. Maybe have them go over to a friend's house to do their school work with them.

Moms, you are engaging in an amazing ministry in the front lines for the souls of your kids! The most important weapon of all is prayer! Pray! Pray! Pray! There is no other way! You won't be able to change their hearts, the circumstance, or some situations in life, but God can and will.

Mom/Dad, be prepared to be changed! God will not only change the kids, He will change you as well . . . if you let Him. I cannot express the joy it brings me to see God's work in both me and my daughter throughout our years of homeschooling. Homeschooling is truly a blessing and an opportunity of a lifetime.

Do you have any ideas for how to homeschool on a budget?

At the moment, my daughter is enrolled in a cyber school which is completely free! If you prefer to use your own curriculum, pray about it and the Lord will provide. He has always provided for us. The first year we were able to get a good discount on our books, and the next two years God connected me with a mom who generously gave me her full curriculum to borrow (the one I actually was planning to buy).

There are many affordable ways to homeschool . . . I have heard people printing free materials off the web, gathering their own books to study and learn, borrowing curricula, buying used books, etc.

How has homeschooling benefitted you or your child so far?

Homeschooling has given me a huge opportunity to disciple my daughter. My daughter told me that she is grateful that I started homeschooling her. She believes if I didn't she would not have accepted Jesus as her Savior. Homeschooling is a great way to bond and to really get to know your child if you desire to and take the time to.

The Lord has blessed our relationship with Him and each other over these past years. She is such a joy in my life! Just to share a few recent events in our house . . . I get a letter from her almost every morning I work, and I also get a note on the front door when I come back home. Many times, she surprises me by making dinner and dessert while I'm at work.

Being a homeschooling mother is challenging work, but it is the best job in the world, and my daughter loves it. I love the moments when we sit and read books together, go for random walks during the warmer weather, play games, or just talk. I love the fact that we control our own schedule and can go on a short trip and take schoolwork along.

Nina Radcliffe

Juice Plus+® distributor; homeschool mom of twelve

My husband and I didn't think we would homeschool. We hadn't heard of it until our church started a homeschool co-op. We liked the idea of being a part of a community that shared the same values as us, and we felt convicted to pass on our faith. We felt the public school curriculum to be questionable also, so we decided to join, and ended up homeschooling ever since. I had a baby about every 18 months, so my children learned how to care for babies, and the older children mentored and helped teach the younger ones.

Do you have any advice for those just starting out?

Don't stress out about academics, even if your child is of high school age. Your focus should to be to raise good adults, not just good students. It's important to teach life skills such as conflict resolution and serving others. Children can practice serving their family and at church to instill selflessness. Currently, I help out in a 2-year-old class at church along with my daughter.

I also recommend giving your child classroom experience through co-ops. My children have participated in a classical school once a week that has helped me avoid burnout and helped my children develop skills like the self-control to sit and listen, have lessons prepared, and develop test-taking skills. My children have grown spiritually through experiences like TeenPact and summer camps.

Lastly, I advise the homeschool parent to take an individual retreat to plan for the homeschool year and spend time with the Lord.

Samantha Sourbeck

Office manager; was homeschooled for 11 years

Many people that know me know that I LOVE to talk! (And that is an understatement.)

The reason I emphasize that I love to talk is because, if you met me right now and started talking to me, you would get the impression I am highly social from public school. Then the famous interrogating question is asked: "Where did you attend school?" (Dun dun dunnnn!!!)

If you can relate, you want to melt and become invisible, tell them you go to the school of your town, or run!

IT'S TRUE . . . I was a homeschooler!

Sometimes it can be challenging to explain to people what homeschooling is. They think you are a deprived child, unsocial, living in a bubble, have never watched TV, or have never been on the Internet before. That was not the case for me. I began homeschooling when I was in 1st grade, and it was the best thing that ever happened to me. My parents chose to homeschool my sister and I because they were called by God to do so, and I am forever grateful they did.

I was super involved with 4-H, the 4-H Performing Arts Club, and Cornell Cooperative Extension financial board, and I avidly volunteered with Operation Christmas Child and any other volunteer opportunity that came my way. I had piano lessons and I was involved with sports such as soccer, fencing, tennis, ice skating, and basketball. I became a soccer referee at the age of 14 (and I still am one). When I graduated high school, I received a refereeing and soccer scholarship along with a 4-H scholarship. My sister graduated high school with scholarships as well and ended up going to California Baptist University for aviation management.

There are endless opportunities for homeschoolers. The key to homeschooling is to get your child the right curriculum or online classes so they can retain the information and love learning about those different subjects. Then they can say, "Wow, I really understand that!" and feel confident taking their tests and quizzes.

If you plan on homeschooling, I highly recommend to parents they get their children involved with their local homeschool groups and 4-H groups. These groups are not just for kids to socialize but also a support team for the teaching parents.

There will always be ups and downs, but the ups always outweighed the downs with homeschooling. I am grateful my parents were patient with me and always showed God's love through teaching me how to behave, speak to people the right way, study hard, how to be honest, always help others, and always go the extra mile in everything I did.

Homeschooling can get exhausting for the parents, but know that your child is always going to remember all the time and hard work you spent making sure their education was the best!

I press on toward the goal to win the prize for which God has called me heavenward in Christ Jesus. (Philippians 3:14)

჻

Wasn't that encouraging to read? So many different families represented here, each with a unique story, a unique set of circumstances, yet all with a common purpose. I love having Samantha's testimony at the end, because it ties together the hope of every homeschool parent. It is the words we all long to hear from our children. She acknowledged her mother's efforts, love, and hard work, and she thrived in her homeschool experience. As parents and teachers at home, our children are the fruit we bear. As homeschooling parents, I pray that we may all give the gift of a committed, nurturing, challenging, and fun-filled experience to our children, and have the hope, peace, and joy that comes from leaning on Jesus each day.

One day when I was feeling frustrated, I began to envision life as a working mom, coveting the satisfaction that can come from a career (like recognition and a paycheck!). God convicted me and allowed me to see that I am working for Him. I should be seeking His praise only (not craving it from people), and all my efforts will not be in vain. As any good dad, He promises to provide for all my needs—I just need to trust in Him, be obedient to what He's called me to, and I will reap an eternal reward.

Homeschooling is not an easy task, but it's a worthy one, and like anything else, it will get easier as you go along. God will give you what you need to keep going. Philippians 4:19 says, "God will supply *every* need of yours according to his riches in glory in Christ Jesus." (ESV)

I know that you can do great things for your household. You CAN homeschool successfully if you choose to! Have faith in yourself as you put your trust in the Lord to give you the strength, and may God reward you fully when He comes again and tells you, "Well done, good and faithful servant!" (Matthew 25:21 ESV)

You CAN do it!

Part III

Resources: Sample Charts and Online Links

I have compiled a list of Internet links in addition to providing you the sample charts promised in Chapter 4. The online links are confirmed to be current at the time of publication. While I hope these will be helpful to you, I can't provide any guarantees for you and your family, so it goes without saying that it's wise to do your own research to back up my suggestions.

There are so many more great resources that I can't possibly list them all, so I hope you'll join our Facebook community (hint: it's the first online link on the list following the chart samples!) to share any updates and point others to resources you find helpful!

To receive free printable copies of these charts, email kmcternanwrites@gmail.com or visit www.mcternan.com.

Comparison Chart

Take notes, recording pros and cons,
so you have a visual list to help you decide.

Topic:	
Positives/benefits:	**Negatives/challenges:**

Other notes:

Student Goal Sheet

Record some goals for the school year (or the summer!),
brainstorm steps to take, and keep track of your progress.

Name:	Year:
Academic:	**Physical:**
Social:	**Spiritual:**
Other notes:	

Internet Resources

Homeschool Community Groups:

Homeschooling: You CAN Do It Facebook page (online):
    https://www.facebook.com/HomeschoolingYouCanDoIt/

Hip Homeschool Moms (online):
    https://www.facebook.com/groups/
    HipHomeschoolMomsCommunity/

Classical Conversations (nationwide):
    https://www.classicalconversations.com/community-search/

Listings of homeschool groups by state or country:
    http://www.home-school.com/groups/

Recommended Extracurricular Club and Activities (Available Nationwide):

4H (positive youth development and mentoring):
    https://4-h.org/

Awana (games, Bible teaching, discipleship):
    https://www.awana.org/

FIRST LEGO League (worldwide):
  http://www.firstlegoleague.org/

Toastmasters International, Youth Leadership Program:
  https://www.toastmasters.org/education/youth-leadership-program

Boy Scouts:
  https://www.scouting.org/

Girl Scouts:
  https://www.girlscouts.org/

American Heritage Girls:
  https://www.americanheritagegirls.org/

Pure Freedom Ministries (purity education resources):
  http://purefreedom.org/free-online-purity-curriculum-coming-soon/

Youth with a Mission (YWAM):
  https://www.ywam.org/

Who to Contact with Homeschool Questions

Homeschool Legal Defense Association; legal advice, homeschool support:
  https://hslda.org/
  Phone: 540-338-5600 (8:30 a.m.–5:00 p.m. ET, Monday–Friday)
  Email contact form: http://hslda.org/contact

Rainbow Resources, Inc.:
  https://www.rainbowresource.com/questions
  Email: info@rainbowresource.com

Phone: 309-695-3200

Live chat: https://rainbowresource.com (click "Live Chat" at top)

Placement Test Resources

Homeschool Testing Services:
https://homeschooltestingservices.com/

Houghton Mifflin's standardized tests:
https://www.hmhco.com/programs/woodcock-johnson

Iowa standardized test:
http://www.bjupresshomeschool.com/category/homeschool-iowa-tests

Stanford standardized test:
http://www.bjupresshomeschool.com/category/homeschool-stanford-tests

Saxon math:
https://www.sonlight.com/homeschool/curriculum/placement-tests/saxon-placement-tests/

Singapore math:
https://www.singaporemath.com/Placement_Test_s/86.htm

Alpha Omega:
https://www.aop.com/placementtests

Sonlight:
https://www.sonlight.com/homeschool/curriculum/placement-tests/

Online Curriculum and Classes:

Veritas:
https://www.veritaspress.com/

Calvert Education:
https://www.calverteducation.com/

Wilson Hill Academy:
http://www.wilsonhillacademy.com/

Apologia online academy:
http://www.apologiaonlineacademy.com/

AIM Academy (a range of middle- and high-school classes
including AP and college credit):
https://debrabell.com/product-category/online-homeschool-
classes/

Liberty University Online Academy (homeschool classes and dual-
enrollment college courses):
https://www.liberty.edu/onlineacademy/

HSLDA (a range of online high school courses, including AP
credits):
https://academy.hslda.org/

Easy Peasy All-In-One Homeschool:
https://allinonehomeschool.com

Freedom Project Academy online school:
http://www.fpeusa.org/

Learning to read:
> http://readingeggs.com/

Science for grades K-12:
> http://www.superchargedscience.com/

Latin:
> https://familystyleschooling.com/latin-andy-login/

Free accredited course on how the brain works (for teens, option to earn college credit!):
> http://brainthriveby25.com/

Curriculum Providers

Rainbow Resource, Inc.:
> https://www.rainbowresource.com/

Christian Book Distributors:
> https://www.christianbook.com/page/homeschool/

Apologia:
> https://www.apologia.com/

Timberdoodle:
> https://timberdoodle.com/

BJU Press:
> http://www.bjupresshomeschool.com/content/home

My Father's World:
> https://www.mfwbooks.com/

Support for Kids with Special Needs

Little Giant Steps (includes free tests on their website):
https://www.littlegiantsteps.com/

National Challenged Homeschoolers Associated Network:
http://www.nathhan.com/

Special Education support listings:
https://hslda.org/content/strugglinglearner/sn_states.asp

Summer Institute for the Gifted:
https://www.giftedstudy.org/

Gifted Homeschoolers Forum:
https://giftedhomeschoolers.org/resources/homeschooling/

Homeschool Family Fun

Many local museums and attractions now offer homeschool days. Ask your local zoo, children's museum, science center, aquarium, botanical garden, art museum, etc., if they have one—and, if they don't, ask them if they'd like to have one!

Hip Homeschool Moms trips:
https://hiphomeschoolmoms.com/category/travel/

Colonial Williamsburg homeschool days:
https://www.colonialwilliamsburg.com/plan/homeschoolers

Six Flags Great Adventure homeschool days:
https://www.sixflags.com/america/special-events/educational-event/2017-home-school-math-and-science-day

Silver Dollar City homeschool weekend:
https://www.silverdollarcity.com/theme-park/Groups/School-Groups/Events/Homeschool-Weekend

Dollywood homeschool days:
https://www.dollywood.com/Groups/Education/Homeschool-Days

SoCal Homeschool Adventures:
https://socalhomeschooladventures.com/

Homeschool Family Camps

Wild and Free:
https://www.bewildandfree.org/

Word of Life:
http://wol.org/

Sandy Cove:
https://www.sandycove.org/

Silver Birch Ranch:
https://www.silverbirchranch.org/camp/

Hartland Christian Camp:
http://www.hartlandcamp.com/programs/home-school-family-camps

Educational Camps

Space camp:
https://www.spacecamp.com/

TeenPact:
   https://teenpact.com/

Nature and science camp:
   http://swiftnaturecamp.com/homeschool-summer-camp

Apologetics camp:
   http://worldview.org/

Digital Media Academy:
   https://www.digitalmediaacademy.org/robotics-and-engineering-camps/

Young Life:
   https://www.younglife.org/Camping/Pages/ForAdults.aspx

Camp Woodward (for action sports):
   http://www.campwoodward.com/

Ohio University Summer Honors Academy:
   (888) 551-6446 or https://www.ohio.edu/summer/

University of Maryland:
   https://oes.umd.edu/

Patrick Henry College:
   (540) 338-1776 or https://www.phc.edu/teen-leadership-camps-the-camps

Homeschool Conferences

Teach Them Diligently:
   https://teachthemdiligently.net/

The Great Homeschool Conventions:
https://greathomeschoolconventions.com/

Summit student conference:
https://www.summit.org/

For a list of homeschool conventions by state:
http://crazyhomeschoollife.com/?s=conventions
(This is a long list—conventions are listed by state, and there are 100 listed outside the U.S. for 2018 alone! This blogger tries to keep this list as exhaustive as possible, so hopefully this search list will pull up future years' lists with no problem.)

Scholarships for Homeschool Families

The Homeschool Foundation:
https://www.homeschoolfoundation.org

About the author

Kirsten McTernan is a homeschooling mom of four boys. Native to Long Island, NY, but raised on three different continents, Kirsten graduated from a boarding school in England before returning to her home country for college. Her background includes public relations and experiential marketing. Kirsten has volunteered at local crisis pregnancy centers, has written the monthly newsletter for Mothers of Preschoolers (www. mops.org) in State College, Pennsylvania, and led a grassroots fundraiser in New York City and Long Island called "Project Backpack." She's passionate about helping women to recognize their God-given abilities and sharing the many exciting benefits of homeschooling. Kirsten loves carrying on the English tradition of "tea-time" daily and has a penchant for boating. She loves collecting friends all over the world, hiking to waterfalls, reading good books, singing with her church worship team, painting, and planning her family's fun night each Friday.

To connect with the author, email kmcternanwrites@gmail.com.

For additional resources, visit www.mcternan.com.

You can also share in Kirsten's online community at www.facebook.com/HomeschoolingYouCanDoIt/.

SELF-PUBLISHING
SCHOOL

NOW IT'S YOUR TURN

Discover the EXACT 3-step blueprint you need to become a bestselling author in 3 months.

Self-Publishing School helped me, and now I want them to help you with this FREE WEBINAR!

Even if you're busy, bad at writing, or don't know where to start, you CAN write a bestseller and build your best life.
With tools and experience across a variety of niches and professions, Self-Publishing School is the <u>only</u> resource you need to take your book to the finish line!

DON'T WAIT!

Watch this FREE WEBINAR now, and
say "YES" to becoming a bestseller:
https://xe172.isrefer.com/go/sps4fta-vts/bookbrosinc4271

Need a cover design? Check out Fiverr!
http://www.fiverr.com/s2/7d090c9ab2

Endnotes

[i] https://www.nheri.org/research-facts-on-homeschooling/
[ii] C.S. Lewis, "Learning in War-Time." *The Weight of Glory*
[iii] https://www.amenclinics.com/about-your-brain/facts-about-your-brain/
[iv] https://www.aop.com/blog/why-colleges-are-recruiting-homeschoolers (italics mine)
[v] https://www.nbcnews.com/feature/college-game-plan/colleges-welcome-growing-number-homeschooled-students-n520126
[vi] http://learninfreedom.org/colleges-home-schooled-students.html
[vii] https://www.homeschoolfoundation.org/index.php?id=340
[viii] https://blog.hslda.org/2015/11/19/ben-carson-homeschool-is-best-for-education/
[ix] http://www.hersheypark.com/groups/schools.php
[x] http://time.com/4572593/increase-depression-teens-teenage-mental-health/
[xi] https://www.cdc.gov/features/safeschools/index.html
[xii] https://www.nbcnews.com/storyline/americas-heroin-epidemic/trump-declares-opioid-crisis-national-emergency-n791576
[xiii] http://www.mtv.com/news/1671547/cyberbullying-sexting-mtv-ap-survey/
[xiv] *Homeschool Progress Report 2009: Academic Achievement and Demographics*
[xv] https://www.nheri.org/homeschool-sat-scores-for-2014-higher-than-national-average/
[xvi] Bolle-Brummond, Mary Beth, & Wessel, Roger D. (2012). "Homeschooled students in college: Background influences, college integration, and environmental pull factors." *Journal of Research in Education*, 22(1), Spring, 2012, 223-249. Retrieved February 29, 2012 from http://www.eeraonline.org/journal/files/v22/JRE_v22n1_Article_10_Wessel.pdf.
[xvii] https://www.hslda.org/research/ray2003/Beyond.asp
[xviii] http://www.businessinsider.com/how-emerson-spartz-built-a-meme-empire-2015-6
[xix] https://www.homeschoolacademy.com/a/famoushomeschoolers/

[xx] http://www.famoushomeschoolers.net/bio_einstein.html#.Weu5kmhSyM8

[xxi] Fölsing, Albrecht, and Ewald Osers. *Albert Einstein: A Biography*. New York: Viking, 1997.

[xxii] http://www.famoushomeschoolers.net/bio_einstein.html#.Weu5kmhSyM8

[xxiii] https://www.nheri.org/research/research-facts-on-homeschooling.html

[xxiv] https://classicalacademicpress.com/what-is-classical-education/

[xxv] https://classicalacademicpress.com/what-is-classical-education/

[xxvi] From their report "Interactions of Top-Down and Bottom-Up Mechanisms in Human Visual Cortex"

[xxvii] http://www.timtebowbill.com/tebow-family

[xxviii] Hamilton, Bethany, Sheryl Berk, and Rick Bundschuh. *Soul Surfer: A True Story of Faith, Family, and Fighting to Get Back on the Board*. New York, NY: Pocket Books, 2012, p. 60-61

CPSIA information can be obtained
at www.ICGtesting.com
Printed in the USA
LVHW080431040122
707786LV00023B/454